THE ROCK CARLING FELLOWSHIP

# 1988

# On caring for the
# national health

THE ROCK CARLING FELLOWSHIP

## 1988

# ON CARING FOR THE NATIONAL HEALTH

### Sir Kenneth Stowe
GCB, CVO

*Principal Private Secretary to
the Prime Minister, 1975–79*

*Permanent Under Secretary,
Northern Ireland Office, 1979–81*

*Permanent Secretary, Department of
Health and Social Security
1981–87*

THE NUFFIELD
PROVINCIAL HOSPITALS
TRUST

Published by the
Nuffield Provincial Hospitals Trust
3 Prince Albert Road, London NW1 7SP
ISBN 0 900574 71 2

Designed by Bernard Crossland
PRINTED IN GREAT BRITAIN BY
BURGESS & SON (ABINGDON) LTD
THAMES VIEW, ABINGDON,
OXFORDSHIRE

# CONTENTS

# ACKNOWLEDGEMENTS

I am grateful to the Nuffield Provincial
Hospitals Trust and to Dr Michael Ashley-Miller,
its Secretary, for encouraging me to think
on these things. I am indebted to many of
my former colleagues for reminding me of
what I had forgotten, and to Mrs Helen
Shirley Quirk for patiently helping me with
this task, and above all to my wife,
who made it possible.

# INTRODUCTION

It is a sound principle that a Permanent Secretary on leaving his Department should—like a vicar vacating his parish—forbear from preaching in it, at it, or about it. My adherence to this principle was challenged when I was invited by the Nuffield Provincial Hospital Trust to accept the Rock Carling Fellowship for 1988, especially since they intimated that they would like the subject of my work to be the management of the National Health Service. I had been much concerned with this during my six years as Permanent Secretary of the Department of Health and Social Security and the Trust hoped I might usefully reflect on that experience—although they were prudent enough to urge that I be not tempted to offer a bland defence of what had been done or attempted.

The temptation to a bland defence is easily resisted. If much was done there remained even more to do; and in any case, Ministers can defend themselves. But as I reflected, under the spur of the Trust's request, on my years as Permanent Secretary I became even more aware that when I was in office that to focus attention on the management of the statutory health authorities is to risk, and perhaps even to make certain, that other and more important considerations relating to the care of the nation's health are overlooked or at least diminished. It is this which persuades me that I might, on this occasion, break the self-denying ordinance and voice my own opinions.

After I received and accepted the Trust's commission, the case for 'a review' of the National Health Service was accepted, and announced by the Government. It is no secret that a very few of us concerned with the future of the NHS had concluded before the General Election of 1987 that we could not go on as we were. The ever-increasing inadequacies exposed in the multiplicity of authorities and agencies; their inflexibilities of structure and complexities of management;

Notes begin on page 80

the mounting excesses of demand over supply; and above all the frustration in the more prosperous parts of the United Kingdom at the failure of Government to endow their local hospital services with some of that prosperity—all of these forced home the realisation that change was needed. So too did the burden of Ministerial involvement in the detail, even minutiae, of NHS management—a burden which Parliament seemed determined to make worse and which a steady increase in the number of Ministers and senior officials and their hours of work seemed never to relieve (1).

The outcome of the review will have been revealed by the time this work appears. So it is not conceived as a contribution to it. Nor is it intended as a work of learning, for I am neither scientist nor scholar. My hope is that these reflections, engendered by a lifetime in the service of government and mainly concerned with its economic and social aspects, will be of some value to those who will carry responsibility hereafter for the many and various facets of caring for 'the national health'.

Perhaps the business of government may eventually be so well-ordered that an incoming team of Ministers or newly-appointed senior officials will have time to acquire a deeper understanding of what is involved in that task before confronting their boxes and in-trays. This collection of notes, reminiscences, and reflections may be useful background for them. Meanwhile they are offered, as my diplomatist friends would say, 'à toutes fins utiles'.

# 1
# Seeing the whole

The national system of health care is extraordinarily complex. Few fields of scientific endeavour are irrelevant to it or wholly free from its impact. Its administration and development invoke the most profound issues of morality, philosophy, and social responsibility. But I know of no single work of reference which accurately describes the whole. I know a few individuals who have managed to acquire—usually over a lifetime—an informed understanding of it. None of them, even those in the highest positions of responsibility, exercises authority over more than a part of it: at the top of the political pyramid, for example, at least seven Secretaries of State carry some responsibility for the health of the nation. Yet there is no field of endeavour that had and has greater need of a breadth of vision.

I have touched 'the care of health' at many different points over the past nearly 40 years. For example:

as a new Assistant Principal in 1951, I had to devil for my elders on two schemes: the payment of expenses for young people with tuberculosis who were sent to Davos in Switzerland for treatment and the refund to poor people of the recently introduced charges for prescriptions, spectacles, and appliances;

nearly 20 years later, when Mrs Judith Hart persuaded the Cabinet to exempt from the increased prescription charge a much wider category of persons if a workable scheme could be devised, I had to find the solution; it still survives as the administrative monstrosity it is, exempting many more people from the charge than ever pay it;

shortly afterwards I was propelled by the Permanent Secretary into reviewing the organisation and staffing of the Department's responsibility for guiding, servicing, and ultimately

Notes begin on page 80

controlling the Health Authorities, then in the form of Regional Hospital Boards and Hospital Management Committees—a responsibility which was manifestly impossible to fulfil within available resources but unavoidable unless Parliament and Government were willing to set the Authorities free;

meanwhile my staff were deep into the intricacies, beyond my understanding, of the system of work-study-based productivity bonus schemes, which the National Board for Prices and Incomes had recommended to improve the earnings of hospital ancillary workers;

more usefully, I was asked to devise the administrative systems for implementing the 1968 Medicines Act provisions to control and approve the production, distribution, and supply of medicines;

as Under-Secretary responsible for Management Services I became embroiled in the computer development programme of the Health Authorities, and in the McKinsey studies which led on to the 1974 re-organisation;

finally, before leaving the Department for nearly 10 years, I was attached to the newly-appointed Chief Scientist, Sir Douglas Black, to assist in the implementation in the health field of the Rothschild Report on Government Research and Development—the customer/contractor/controller principle of blessed memory.

This miscellany of episodes—not, of course, selected entirely at random—will serve perhaps to point up some of the wider issues embedded in our health care system—the redundancy created by medical advances (2); the administrative nonsense that is bequeathed by party political dogma; the impossibility of reconciliation between the Government's need to control and the practitioners' need for freedom of action; the price of the monolithic semi-skilled, and lowly-paid labour force on which the hospital service has come to depend; the safety, efficacy, availability, and price of medicines; the always enticing but so unrewarding prospect of re-organisation and 'modernisation'; and the failure over four decades to find an acceptable and workable means of investigating objectively the delivery of health services and applying the lessons learned.

I saw little evidence then of a wider view when these and similar episodes occurred—not in Parliament, nor in Government, nor in 'the Health Service' itself. Nor can I exonerate myself—we always wore the blinkers necessary to make any progress at all down difficult paths. When I was sent back to the Department as Permanent Secretary in 1981, there was little difference: the pre-occupation was still with the hospital authorities. This might seem reasonable: most of the Government's money spent on health care is spent in hospitals, and the highest levels of clinical treatment are provided by them. Other factors have and no doubt will put the hospital service into continuing prominence. But there is more to it than that.

Health care, including of course, care for ill-health, is so vast and complex a subject that those engaged in giving it are increasingly very specialised indeed. They are also, in general, highly motivated and committed to their special discipline, skill, or subject. Taking a broad view is not their normal approach. Each and every specialism or discipline generates a lobby among those who practice it, commonly supported by those who benefit or hope to benefit from their services.

Government, by contrast, has an obligation to hold an overview of health care itself, in all its forms, and of its other responsibilities alongside health care. It is thereby put immediately at a disadvantage. Very few of those engaged in health care will openly support a preference over their own interest for sound money, secure defence, or the maintenance of law and order: yet each is a pre-requisite for good health care. And even in the field of health care their discordant voices cry for preferences. Since the bulk of the specialisms and their practitioners are in the hospitals, it is the hospital service provided by Health Authorities which constitutes the most powerful lobby or cluster of lobbies in health care, and which largely dictates therefore the agenda for debate about inadequacies and the measures and resources needed to make them good.

Therein lies the origin of successive Governments' involvement in what is usually described as 'the re-organisation of the

NHS', a process which has been about to happen, happening, or has just happened these past four decades. Alongside the issues of structure, organisation, and management of the hospital service which this opens up, there are the issues of its capital building programme, of the revenue resources for the current and subsequent years, and, of course, the cost of the pay-bill for its UK workforce of nearly one million people.

Much of the debate about health in the post-IMF era (from 1977 onwards) has been dominated by the interests and resources of the hospital authorities (3): in consequence it has been largely a debate about institutions and their staff, their funding and their management. The ends of good health care, and how best to attain them tend to be squeezed out, because Ministers and their most senior officials are pre-occupied with the central Government responsibility for the Health Authorities. More on this later. Meanwhile, by way of illustration, here are some matters which, on reflection and with hindsight, I wish had been more thoroughly addressed during my years as Permanent Secretary:

Education for good health and self-help.
Medicines and self-medication.
The respective roles of the different clinical professions.
Medical education, the role of the universities; and of the teaching hospitals.
Research and development.
The caring community and its renewal.
An aged and ageing population.
The voluntary sector.
Representing the patient's interests.

The reminiscences and reflections which follow will not, of course, overlook the necessary care which the hospital authorities and their one million employees provide, but they will, I hope, serve to illuminate the whole a little better. First, however, we must clear away one or two myths and illusions.

# 2

# Of myth and illusion

One man's myth is another's most cherished belief; one man's illusion is another's fond hope or expectation. I fear, therefore, that I shall offend in what follows.

The myths surround the idea of a National Health Service, its origins and its creation: conceived, so it is held, in 1942 in the Beveridge Report; constructed 1945–48 and instituted in largely its present form by a Labour Government whose claim to proprietorship is passionately defended; a new and unique edifice which could not have been built in any other way; the envy of the world.

No-one who grew up before the Second World War and saw what ill-health could do to a poor family could doubt the compelling necessity for better and comprehensive health care (4). But is it quite true that the Beveridge Grand Design was the only way? My graduation from faithful believer to sceptic began 25 years ago when, as a young Principal, I had to dig into the origins of the Beveridge Report in the social security field, with particular reference to the concept of the poverty line and the problem of rent, on which he and a distinguished Fellow of the Royal Statistical Society, R. F. George, laid the foundations of the National Insurance and Social Assistance schemes (5). I was not impressed. I came back to these doubts when in 1983–84 we had to initiate the review of the Social Security system to prevent its ultimate collapse, while wrestling with the intractability of raising from tax revenue more resources for the hospital and community health services. The concurrent debate within the Department about 'alternative methods of financing health care', which Patrick Jenkin had initiated when he was Secretary of State for Social Services, re-inforced the case for fresh thinking.

State-supported health care for individuals, given in return

Notes begin on page 80

for a weekly insurance premium, and administered by independent 'approved societies', had been introduced in 1911. It was well-established, and had been already extended by the Second World War, covering 20·3 m workers, 43 per cent of the population. It offered a working base on which to develop. Instead, that justifiable and properly 'insurable' approach to health care was subsumed into a comprehensive 'national insurance' pensions and benefits scheme which was from the outset inadequate for its purposes and in no sense 'insurable'. Beveridge effectively hi-jacked National Health Insurance for the purposes of income-redistribution. The retention of a notional National Health Insurance element in the N.I. contribution was a meaningless sop—no Government has ever been able to use it as a means of providing significant resources for health care because the National Insurance base on which it rested was already so large, and growing so much larger in prospect, that it could not be further enlarged without damage to the economy (6).

Over and above this, the edifice of 1948 rested upon an act of nationalisation which is rarely described as such and which I doubt would even begin to be marketable today—the taking into the possession of the State (formally into the possession of the Secretary of State for Health) of the hospitals of all kinds which had been built and serviced mainly at their own expense by preceding generations of local people. Thus, at a stroke, was the gulf created between each community and its hospitals, the bridging of which has called forth much—and largely ineffective—ingenuity ever since. And the consequence of this all-too-evident failure has been the continuing, usually covert, search for some device, whereby the responsibility for essentially local institutions could be transferred back to the community which they should serve—see the Hidden Agenda.

The consequence of the abandonment of a health insurance approach in 1946, politically compelling as the case may have been, is that the 'customer' of health care in the UK, the individual citizen or patient, has always been kept down; supplicant rather than purchaser. Which in turn means that he has become dependent upon the State, i.e. the Exchequer, to act as his purchaser and upon Parliament to defend his interest*. And so to the illusion.

It may be unlikely, in the foreseeable future, that we shall move away from the concept of an Exchequer-financed health service for the generality of people. The judgements of yesterday's Royal Commission and today's eminent authorities argue against it. They do so because of the illusion that all Government need do to make the original (and perfect?) conception work is to put more money into it; that sooner or later Government will do so under the pressure of public opinion, on a scale large enough to make good potentially all the deficiencies; and that the deficiencies will then *in fact* be made good by the new managerial competence with which the hospital authorities are now endowed. If only they were right.

The illusion extends further: when, not if, Government comes up with the extra cash, then the growing and deplorable tendency to 'centralisation and intervention' can be reversed. I am, I believe, credited (or discredited) with some responsibility for centralising and intervening. It was and is clear to me that nearly 100 per cent Exchequer financing must entail rigorous oversight of where, and how, the money goes. A rudimentary knowledge of English history will indicate that sooner or later Parliament will jib at signing cheques without investigating their use. The welcome, and overdue, construction of the National Audit Office has given the Public Accounts Committee the necessary tool of investigation and they will not fail to use it (7).

In consequence, the Secretary of State and the Accounting Officer especially, have to measure up to their responsibilities of ensuring that the management process at all levels in the health care system delivers value for money—for patient and taxpayer. That process has barely begun. It will indeed be an illusion to suppose that Central Government can back off unless and until some other source of funding can be established, e.g. by insurance provision, with the insurers being the intervening third party.

---

* Or, if you really are a starry-eyed optimist, on the Community Health Councils!

There is, of course, a powerful (or at least powerfully emotional) case against insurance-based provision for health care. Health care is different because the customer paying his insurance premiums cannot know what service he needs. In that respect he differs from every other customer, insured or not, who thinks he knows what he wants or wants done. Thus the equation of the patient with the customer is flawed. So it is, so long as the customer is seen as an isolated entity. But some remedy lies in the combination of customer/patient *interests* in a collective *power* to purchase, which is exercised on their behalf by those competent to do so. If the Exchequer-financed system is to continue, then there should follow a separation of responsibility for purchasing services on behalf of patients from responsibility for providing them—preferably in competition with other providers and, therefore, always costed and priced. This is a necessary pre-condition for effectiveness.

One of the most encouraging consequences of the recent hammering, in the 1980s, of the Health Authorities on the anvil of public expectation has been the recognition of this distinction and its growing acceptance as an urgent target. There are already various models identified, and being debated, for separating purchaser and provider responsibility, and I shall be disappointed if my former colleagues fail to come up with better—and more workable. As an act of self-indulgence I here record my own preference for starting with costed out-patient and day-patient services, with the bill going to the patient's general practitioner for authorisation, and then on to the Family Practitioner Committee for payment and selective post-audit. Whatever methods and services are chosen, the solution will, however, prove to be yet another illusion unless the provider knows his costs and the purchaser has the option of paying a competitive price to a provider of his choice. Most important of all is to establish and apply the principle that whatever the purchase and whoever the purchaser and provider, there must be rigorous value-for-money audit.

But, of course, the percipient reader will immediately have seen the trap: by what authority and by reference to what criteria can any entity, however distinguished its members, exercise 'purchasing power' on behalf of patients? The besetting sin of the health care system for as long as I have known it is its patronising attitude to the public: assumed to be ignorant and expected to be docile. Are they? This brings me to what ought to be the starting point of a continuing debate.

# 3

# I can do more for myself than you think I can

A population which can increasingly utilise private capital to house itself; cope with the complexities of urban traffic control; drive on the wrong side of the European road network, and look forward to a Channel Tunnel; manipulate or at least survive the daily commuter tidal flows; invest in and use an array of hi-tech equipment to better its home environment physically and for entertainment; complete all the documentation necessary for driving licences, for personal insurance on goods and lives, and for football pools; and demonstrate every day a massive concern for the well-being of itself and for the population at large is or ought to be highly capable of caring for its own health, either by prevention or by remedy. I doubt if we have given them anywhere near the information or opportunity to realise their potential.

Education and instruction in self-care—invest in more and better of each and the pay-back should be enormous and profitable. Unfortunately, it is not straightforward.

Health education has a long and creditable history. Much of it was and thankfully still is undertaken by concerned individuals and voluntary organisations, not by the State in any of its manifestations. That is much to be preferred for two simple reasons (8). First, there seem rarely to be absolute certainties in health care advice—the do's and don'ts, once past a very limited range of specific subjects, tail off into ever finer qualifications. Don't smoke is negative, absolute and easy; so are don't drink and drive, and don't sniff glue. But once beyond the negative and the absolute, life gets difficult. Don't drink too much; eat less or eat less fatty foods; take more exercise; breast-feed the baby if you can and if you and the baby like it; don't have sexual intercourse with strangers

Notes begin on page 81

—or not too many strangers, and not in too many ways, and if you must use a condom. Not much certainty in all that.

The second reason follows from it. The role of Government, here as elsewhere, is best confined to essentials and to certainties: the equivocal or simple disquieting message is best avoided by Government: it will inevitably provoke probing if not hostile criticism and the uncertainty, not the message, is what comes across. An illustration: is *butter* good for you, bad for you, or don't know? There were great and predictable ructions when some experts wanted the Government's booklet on healthy eating to condemn butter-eating as a bad thing and were met with resistance by Government itself. Wisely, in my view, the experts saw the merit of being less than absolute before Parliament forced the uncertainty out of them (9).

The uncertainty—and therefore, the case for Government keeping a distance—is even greater when clinical advice tangles with social, moral, and philosophical issues. The obvious example is the field of sexually transmitted diseases. It is not AIDS, and the infamous posters that I have in mind, though they illustrate the point clearly enough. Sexually transmitted diseases were one of the growing diseases in the UK before anyone in the Department had ever mentioned AIDS to me or to Ministers. That was a pointer to the risks of a sexually promiscous society, and the creation of the environment in which AIDS developed, but a campaign against promiscuity was not a cause Ministers could have taken up.

The case for keeping a distance is not, however, to be seen as a case for abdication. On the contrary, it argues for Government locating the necessary resources for health education outside Government and then giving its moral and political support as necessary. The establishment of the Health Education Authority is, I hope, a step forward in this direction. It was Norman Fowler who conceived the idea of making the new Authority the '15th Regional Health Authority', thereby bringing it a status in the system which its remit merited. This was meant to—and I trust will—reverse a sad retreat brought about by the misdirection of itself on the part of the former Health Education Council and its officers. They succumbed to the disease of the nanny state—demanding that Government '*do something*' (some would really have liked, I believe, to have made smoking a criminal offence), and misguidedly believing that Government would be more likely to 'do something' if the message was conveyed through a loud-hailer across town.

That is not to say that the Health Education Authority should be subservient or draw back from giving advice which Ministers would not want to give or might even prefer were not given at all. There will be differences of view and of emphasis. And the health education responsibility can be effectively discharged only by a body prepared to stand by its convictions in its advice to the public. Its advice to Government is best given quietly; and with understanding that because Governments commonly feel obliged to compromise, it is good argument alone which will dissuade them.

It will, I believe be a continuing high priority in health care for Government to ask more of the HEA, and to expect of it intelligent and sensitive exploration of health education using, as far as possible, interests, bodies, and individuals outside Government and Government's satellite Authorities. And that means giving them resources to purchase staff of the highest quality, to investigate the effectiveness of educational programmes, and above all to explore the potential to take health education truly into the field of self-care, including using and exploiting commercial interests to the benefit of the public health—for example, in self-medication.

# 4

# On taking medicine

Medicines seem always to be a source of political or professional outrage or embarrassment. Thus, they are taken too often, prescribed in too large quantity, wasted by patients and/or doctors, too costly, too dangerous, and exploited by the pharmaceutical industry at the expense of other needs of health care. From the introduction of the prescription charge in 1951, and the calculated Ministerial resignations which followed, through to the imposition of the limited list of generic drugs on professional prescribing, and in every annual review of public expenditure, they have been a high point of controversy.

It should not be a matter of surprise, nor of too serious concern that patients like medicines. The earliest forms of treating the sick were by medicine. There is a growing not diminishing interest in the revival and use of traditional remedies in the developed as well as in the developing countries. And the most superficial acquaintance with medical practice will expose the continuing benefit which the sick get from the placebo effect, from unconventional and 'unscientific' medicine, and from healing by faith. Were it not so, there would be little case for the double blind randomised controlled trial of current practice.

What is too little understood is the desire for and practice of self-medication, and the willingness to pay for it among the public at large. One of the most useful lessons about the health care system in the UK is to be had free by standing awhile near the pharmacy counter of any retail chemist. The trade in 'patient' medicines is immense. It has gone a long way beyond the barking of the quack and the charlatan. The credit for this goes to the Medicines Act 1968—a vitally important social reform which, by the institution of a licensing system for the

Notes begin on page 82

production and sale of medicines under the direction of the Medicines Commission, has removed thousands of useless or dangerous substances from the pharmacy counter and enhanced the availability of medicines of proven safety and efficacy. I have never incidentally heard a Minister or party political activist claim any credit for this or for the fact that in this system the UK now has a model much-admired by the world at large.

The consequence has been that the local pharmacy has developed into the real first line of health care. The traffic through it each day exceeds that through GPs' surgeries. Many of the medicines bought are what the GP would have prescribed and the level of advice from the pharmacist plainly, by observation, commands much confidence from this immense public willing to spend its own money on readily available remedies. The introduction of the limited list of generic drugs prescribable for certain indications has, though not designed for the purpose, taken this a stage further: the pharmacist can say that a particular medication available over the counter is exactly the same as what the GP could have prescribed under the NHS if consulted in his surgery and perhaps cheaper: and no appointment is necessary.

The consultative status of the pharmacist is further advanced by the sensible practice of making another category of medicines available 'in pharmacy only', i.e. the pharmacist personally not the counter assistant must authorise the purchase (without, be it noted, any paperwork—a model worthy of emulation). The effect is, again, to make professional advice more widely available and bring it closer to the individual who wants to meet his requirements as quickly as possible and is prepared to pay the over-the-counter price rather than the prescription charge per item—and it may even be lower. It also reduces the pressure on the GP system (10).

It is further advanced again by the increasing availability of high-quality written advice in the form of professionally prepared leaflets about specific conditions, some common some not. Some of these leaflets come from authority, e.g. the Family Practitioner Committee, some from independent bodies like the Health Education Authority, some from manufacturers. They enhance the ability of the literate customer to get sensible advice which can be read and re-read rather than have to be absorbed first time in a conversation (11).

This brings us, of course, to the threshold of inter-professional rivalry. The Pharmaceutical Society of Great Britain would like to extend the development of pharmacy-based health care by giving the professionally-qualified pharmacist authority to provide a wider range of medicines. They are not alone in their ambition to make inroads into the GPs' 'monopoly' of prescribing powers. The Community Nurses would similarly like to have authority to prescribe medication in straightforward cases. Neither of those claims is irresponsible or motivated by a desire for greater remuneration (though, life being what it is, that would certainly be expected to follow). The Clucas Committee and the Cumberlege Committee, dealing with the role of the pharmacist and with community nursing respectively, have explored these areas. They merit serious consideration, starting from what is likely to be in the best interests of an increasingly literate and informed population (12).

These reflections could easily be misunderstood as hostile to the GP, seeking to dilute his responsibility and/or devalue his professional skill. Not at all. It is rather a case for recognising the value to us all of the demystification of much to do with medicines and their uses, and for relieving a highly-trained doctor from a volume of consultation that does not call for that kind of training. And it may enhance the feasibility of extending the role of the general practitioner into clinical areas which currently fall within the responsibility of the hospital—a process already taking place, e.g. in respect of minor surgical and other procedures. It does, of course, call for the highest professional and scientific standards from the pharmacists and the community nurses. It requires the same from the suppliers of medicine—in our case from one of the most successful industries in the UK, and one of the bogeys of the NHS polemicists: the pharmaceutical industry.

# 5

# On making medicine

The pharmaceutical industry was not nationalised in 1948 (13). I find this remarkable—and give thanks for it. What emerged instead—by a piece of administrative ingenuity for which I can claim no credit but which I have long admired—was a voluntary agreement on a price mechanism between a single controlled market and a miscellany of suppliers to that market. The medical profession has in general freedom to prescribe any product of the suppliers but the suppliers have to compete for its custom and accept a constraint on their overall profitability.

This scheme—now the PPRS (14)—is from time to time anathematised in Parliament, by health service lobbyists and by the media. It has, of course cost the health budgets more, perhaps a lot more, than if available medicines had been purchased at the lowest price in the world market and doctors' powers of prescribing were limited to a small range of drugs or a finite budget. There would however then have been another and different price to pay. The logical (and ideological) consequence would have been the establishment of a national drugs purchasing agency to secure the supply at bulk prices; and a national warehousing and distribution network. (I forbear from speculating what follies this would have compounded in the NHS supplies and storage system). I would not have relished the Accounting Officer's role. More importantly, the UK would not now be the possessor of an industry which adds just under £1bn p.a. to our balance of payments from overseas sales, invests £700m p.a. in research and development, and employs 87,000 people directly (of whom 20–25 per cent are graduates) in the research sector operating at the frontiers of medical science. It has developed

Notes begin on page 82

under UK patents about half of the top 20 drugs, measured by volume, prescribed under the NHS.

I spent many hours arguing indirectly with the National Audit Office and the Treasury and giving evidence to the Public Accounts Committee on the issue of drug supply and pricing (15). The present system is not perfect, and fertile minds will go on inventing new (and untested) alternatives. It is, however, economical in administration, although as in other areas I think we could usefully have bought in more financial expertise from the private sector to help us. But the system works and is flexible. It is in my judgement a good example of how a state-owned purchasing monopoly can exercise its economic power to extend and develop a competitive market in which the supplier has an incentive to efficiency in quality and availability and, where patents have expired, in price. And, be it noted, the purchaser (the GP) can be distinguished from the supplier (the pharmaceutical company).

The concept is sound in principle—and worthy of extension in the health care system generally, subject to the two lessons learned the hard way in recent years. First that complete freedom to purchase is unnecessarily costly in areas where the clinical evidence clearly points to satisfactory standard products—the 'limited list' of generic medicines. Secondly, that the financial authorities (in this case the Prescription Pricing Authority and the Family Practitioner Committees) have an obligation to monitor purchasing requirements and to constrain excess or inadequacy; and with information technology of a modest standard they have the means to do it. If a real internal market in hospital care can be developed, the experience with medicines offers useful guidance: the purchaser distinguished from the supplier, with the responsibility for purchasing put at the lowest operational level, and selectively post-audited.

The system for the provision of medicines still suffers, however, from a lack of real incentive on the part of patient or prescriber to use as few medicines as possible as economically as possible. Indeed, the patient has a built-in incentive (his own convenience) to try anything and to have as large a supply as possible if it is free; and the practitioner has little by the way of leverage against this except his own authority. This enhances—or does not inhibit—the proper growth in the use of medicines which pharmaceutical research has made possible. The drug bill, being demand-related and not cash-limited has, in consequence grown to a size which is disproportionate in relation to other and equally pressing social requirements; and the Treasury have no option but to seek to put a fence round it. If a more rational system of charging can be introduced in place of the present absurdity, progress might be made: otherwise other constraints are inevitable. These will not necessarily be better or more effective but they will be likely to create not only conflict with the clinical independence of practitioners, but an even bigger bureaucracy too.

# 6

# On giving and helping

The medicine-men and women are but one end of the spectrum of essential support for health care outside the state-financed system. At the other, and equally important although less attended to, are 'the givers and helpers', the volunteers of goods, cash, and services: an enormous army of men and women in groups and organisations of infinite variety whose work underpins the whole system.

I have never encountered, on entering a Department store in the High Street or a petrol service station, or a supermarket, or a restaurant or hotel, a plaque on the wall recording that the service itself or the amenity was or is provided by gifts from friends or the work of volunteers. It is however a common-place that every hospital or clinic in the UK has such plaques or notices, usually several of them. The volume of voluntary giving and helping in health care is a remarkable pheno-menom. The extent of it is rarely discussed. Indeed, I cannot recall a single occasion during my years in the Department of Health or elsewhere in Government when the role of the voluntary sector, its potential and its possible development, was seriously considered as an issue of policy worthy of the attention of senior officials and their Ministers.

This was not because we were wholly unaware of what is done. The evidence is strikingly obvious wherever one visits; some of it in the most unlikely, unrewarding, or unattractive environments. I recall, for example, the League of Friends of Rampton Hospital, and the Salvation Army's de-toxification unit at their hostel in Whitechapel. On a grander scale there is the blood-donor system, the hospital car service, and the hospice movement (16). On the personal level, there is infinite variety in the little trolley shops pushed round the hospital

Notes begin on page 83

21

wards by volunteers; and even more personal the ex-cancer patients visiting the new cancer patients in hospital to reassure and advise. At the technical level, a vast array of advanced equipment has been installed by the efforts of local fund-raisers.

None of this can be priced, except in the sense that the cost of a piece of equipment is known, as is the hourly cost of a particular service bought in the labour market. Much of it is not, in fact, replaceable by authority if the voluntary giving were withheld. And even if it were replaceable, the public expenditure priorities would stop short of some, if not most, of these endeavours.

The scale and diversity of all this, and its implications, should be central to any thinking about the future of the health care of this country. The willingness of supply is a healthy reminder, if one were needed, that health care in all its many dimensions is seen as belonging to the people in a community, not to a District, still less a Regional Health Authority. The innovations brought about by enterprising 'volunteers'—I think especially of the hospice movement —are both a rebuke and a challenge to those who could have, and should have foreseen and provided for the needs of a community. The history of medical advances in the UK is commonly of charities filling the gaps or meeting a growing need until eventually Government wakes up to its responsibilities. The givers and helpers, especially in the near-irreplaceable services—blood supply and hospital car service —merit continuing support to maintain their well-being. Even an invitation to a Royal Garden Party or to a hospital opening ceremony would go a long way.

There is, of course, a danger: that the 'voluntary' service will be assumed by Government, or by any of its many agencies in health care, to be readily available in substitution for publicly-funded and staffed services for which there are now no or inadequate resources. This has been a continuing and proper concern of the voluntary movement and the lead organisation in it, the National Council of Voluntary Organisations. And one should admit that from their point of view, this substitution seems to have happened, particularly in the field of community care for the mentally ill and the mentally handicapped. An ambulance drawing up near a voluntary hostel and the driver telling the patient to walk to it and seek admission; and the mentally-ill patient discharged from hospital by taxi (fare-paid) similarly to knock without notice on the door of a voluntary home: these stories can be vouched for. They are not all that unusual, and reflect no credit on the statutory authorities or on the implementation of what is or ought to be a positive and commendable policy for care in the community.

The willingness to give is not, inevitably, an unmixed blessing for the recipient agencies. It is human to want to see what one gives, so there is a preference for providing hardware or buildings—leaving the normally higher running costs to be borne by the recipient. This phenomenon is not unique to health care but it hits harder. Health care is so labour intensive that there always will be pressure on running costs, and gifts that ignore them compound the problem. There is some recognition of this, in the medical research charities especially, and it needs to be encouraged. But that, again, requires a much more intimate relationship with and care about the voluntary movement than has been achieved so far.

There is an urgency about the promotion and nourishment of 'giving and helping' which puts it high on my agenda for consideration by all concerned with the care of the national health, starting with Government but most certainly not stopping there. The reason for urgency is not simply that exchequer-finance will not be sufficient to do what is required, but because what is required is beyond the capacity of authority to deliver, particularly so in facing the problems of a society with a big and growing population of the disabled, the frail, and the very old.

# 7

# Of mortality

Tables of data relating to morbidity and mortality, analysed by reference to many and various social, geographical, economic, and industrial, etc. characteristics, are the stuff of epidemiology, which is or should be the science at the heart of public health care. Their analysis points the way to preventable illness and premature, because preventable, death. Countless lobbies and pressure groups have come into existence as a result of this kind of study, seeking resources and research to ascertain the causes and incidence of the particular illness or disease, and its prevention, cure, or alleviation.

I doubt if there is a known figure for the number of these bodies, even in the UK. They seem to be growing inexorably. Their very existence often implies criticism of the professions for not taking their particular interest more seriously, and of Government for not having given extra or at least ear-marked funds for the purpose. No Minister or MP or Peer can ever appear to be unsympathetic. So the relentless pressure for more resources is reinforced, the facts packaged in emotion to make an impressive case.

All of this is predictable and has to be lived with. It tends, however, to help divert our minds from the one fact that is central to our responsibility for a caring community. We shall all die. Our human mortality rate is still 100 per cent and bound to remain so. This is not the kind of observation one would be thanked for if offered as a contribution to the Debate on The Queen's Speech, a Ministerial statement, or even a reply to a PQ. It is not the stuff of politics, which has to be about tomorrow and the prospect of a better tomorrow at that.

We have not been very good at facing up to this—the hospice movement has, but it is a shining example of honesty and far-sightedness which owed little or nothing to the State in its inception. Nor have we done very well in facing up to *the* factor which will dominate health for decades to come: the growth in the numbers and attendant frailties, of the very elderly. The problem was not wholly unforeseen. The Philips Committee on economic and financial problems of the provision for old age was set up as long ago as 1954, when Government first tried to come to terms with the fact that the 'Welfare State', so-called, was unviable in the form in which it was established. The demographic projections have followed steadily in its wake, indicating the likely volume of the very old. But we seem consistently to under-estimate the rate of survival and therefore the consequences for care and the carers, and the costs. This is hardly surprising: no previous generations in the history of the UK have experienced the massive upsurge in elderly dependancy of all kinds which is now upon us. That dependency is likely to get bigger as the years pass unless medical science can truthfully be said to 'add life to years rather than just add years to life'.

# 8

# A caring community

Meanwhile, the community has to cope with an increasingly aged population (17) which includes an infinite range and complexity of dependency upon the help of others in a bewildering variety of circumstances. As is usual, the reaction of Government is, because it has to be, to search for structures and models which will at least contain the problem, hopefully ameliorate it, do so at reasonable cost and with proper value for money, and above all demonstrate that Government is doing something.

I long ago concluded that it is not in the gift of Government to construct still less to direct a caring community. It seems bound, judging by experience, to fall into either or both of two traps. First, Government has to act through a legislative framework of one kind or another. Its prescription for civic virtue—another way of describing what constitutes a caring community—will be uniform and as a result either prescriptive and regulatory in fine detail, or only enabling in the most general terms. The Social Security system of income-tested benefits exemplifies the former; the local authority powers to provide social services the latter. Each can work up to a point; neither can deliver a comprehensive—or comprehensible—response to a need which is so often beyond practical definition in general terms.

Secondly, Government will always be bound to prescribe the highest standards, when something far less than best would be a substantial advance; and to put the professions in a central and often controlling position, when lesser skills would demonstrably go a long way to meet the need. This is not an attack on quality nor on the medical and social work professions. The point is general. Lady Wagner's Committee

Notes begin on page 83

on (18) residential care, in its otherwise admirable report, fell into this second trap, with the best of motives, by specifying a social work qualification for the 'manager' of a residential home rather than a level of personal quality and commitment, competence, and experience, which is not quite the same thing.

If a caring community is to do better than our present inadequate best then it has somehow to enlist for millions of individuals in undescribable varieties of circumstance the support needed to do for them the humdrum things we would prefer to do for ourselves. The support can come from any or all of:

   families living with or near the person in need of support;
   friends and neighbours;
   local voluntary workers, from church, club or charity;
   local authority-provided social services by way of meals, shopping and other facilities;
   the community nurse;
   the general practitioner; and a chiropodist;
   the corner shop and the nearest pharmacy;
   the local constable;
   the itinerant tradesman—in milk, window cleaning, posts and transport.

I recite this trite catalogue of requirements and resources only because the obvious message it conveys seems so often, and almost wilfully to be ignored. The need cannot be met by Government, nor by Authority. Yet we had in 1987 an Audit Commission report—one of the worst-informed and most ill-judged analyses I ever read—proposing a massive re-organisation of benefits and services in a new structure which could only, in my view, confuse and delay progress. I was sad to see the subsequent Report on Community Care repeating this pre-occupation with structure, financial redistribution, and controlling authority—although it did recognise the need for intensely local support (while making the error of supposing that the unemployed and the school-leavers should somehow be enjoining to provide much of it).

I have spent much of my life in Government engaged in either confronting the intractable or re-organising something —and all too often, the latter is grasped as the panacea for the former*. The problem of securing adequate or even practical support in their own homes for those whose lives are wrecked without it—recognising that only most, not all, are very old—seems intractable. It cannot be so: the number of successful ventures proves that. It looks formidably expensive to address it comprehensively—yet *the* essential requirement is no more than face-to-face contact by an interested person who can use a telephone and know whom to call. It seems superficially attractive to think in terms of one local 'authority' with the resources to buy the whole range of services— from a window-cleaner to a residential home—for each individual needing care. But that authority will never be acceptable as an arbiter of their fate by a population who are, however frail, characterised by fierce independence. Nor, with respect to my fellow officials, will it ever be truly competent to do its job well.

The solutions (note the plural) must lie elsewhere. In the hearts and minds of each community, be it a terrace-row, a street, a block, or wherever. How? I do not know, beyond saying that the idea of a Welfare State solution must first be displaced. In its place we must nourish the idea of a well-caring and well-cared for community, in which the next step towards any solution is DIY. Because it is so remarkable, unprecedented, and so uplifting in this context, I cite as an example of the right attitude Lady Wagner's Committee setting up its own post-report development group of all interested parties, to bring about, *without authority, and without government money*, the betterment in residential care that is so much desired.

We are, of course, addressing these problems late in the day. And I wince at the recollection of how much time and effort in Central Government has been deployed elsewhere, on lesser matters, or matters which should have been managed without the involvement on such a massive scale of the time

---

* Re-organisation is the ready refuge of the tired mind—anon.

and energy of Ministers and senior officials. I think especially of our failure to achieve the benefits of good relevant research into health and care services and our necessary pre-occupation with the successive re-organisations (note the plural again) of the hospital authorities, with their management, and with their personnel. Let's take research first.

# 9

# Investigation and invention

The State has been supporting the Medical Research Council (MRC) since the First World War for the purposes of medical, i.e. scientific and clinical research. There is a complex and powerful structure starting with the Advisory Board for Research Councils and ending with the Systems Boards of the MRC and the process of peer review, to supervise and direct this expenditure. There is a complementary structure of medical and related research in the medical schools and other Departments of universities, funded by the UGC and also supported by the MRC and including some of the MRC's units. There is a third and increasingly important source of resources and direction for medical research in the medical research charities, who now give more money for it than the State provides through the MRC. There is a fourth arm in the shape of the R&D effort of the pharmaceutical industry amounting again to more money than is spent by the MRC but in this case provided from the industries profits and, therefore, indirectly financed in part by the public expenditure cost of medicines in the NHS (19).

Tucked into this complex array of authorities, institutions, and resources is the frail specimen called Health Services Research, for which provision has been made in Department of Health budgets since the early 1950s. For the decade since 1977, the health services research budget has ranged between £10 m and £20 m p.a. In 1987–88, it was £12·9 m. The idea behind it was admirable: to enable the responsible Department to commission investigations into the delivery and effectiveness of health services so as to ensure (or at least promote) their greater effectiveness. Much time and effort was put into developing a useful programme of research projects into areas of

Notes begin on page 84

particular difficulty and in building up the Departmental equivalent of the MRC 'units', of which some 34 were created eventually. But 'health services research' never seemed to develop into a significant force, in the Department or in health care authorities or in the world of scientific research itself (20).

The reasons for this are not very clear. One factor was undoubtedly the appalling diversion of effort into implementing the Government's (Rothschild) White Paper policy on R&D, under which the MRC funds for research were 'transferred' to the Department, which was then expected to function as a 'customer' and commission research from 'contractors' operating under the 'controller' MRC (21). The only reason for remembering this folly (it was reversed when the funds were transferred back again in 1980 under a concordat still in place) is that it marks so clearly the confusion of thought surrounding the role of the central Department, and its capability for it.

Another factor was, and I think always will be, the constraint on resources, especially of high-quality manpower, available for centrally-commissioned health services research. This must in part be inherent in the nature of the subject—it is not 'pure' science like the academic study of some aspect of medicine. It is 'applied' science certainly, but it often hardly merits the name science at all, being essentially the pragmatic analysis of effective or ineffective services (and not so far removed from good O&M at that) to secure best value-for-money and optimal use of resources.

Yet if this is what it is about, one stumbles on the inevitable difficulty of involving Ministers in the subject. The problem is circular: for want of such involvement and direction the programme, such as it is, disconnected itself from the mainstream of Ministerial interests. And it then committed its resources so far ahead that it had no capacity to engage in the more immediate issues which necessarily engage Ministerial attention. It has also to be said that Ministers are not always avid to acquire the relevant information by objective enquiry before committing themselves to a point of view—but if the objective enquiry would take so long as to be irrelevant, their position is understandable and has my sympathy.

In the result, I know of no strategic issue with which Ministers were concerned during my time as Permanent Secretary which was illuminated by the Health Services Research Programme. Illumination there was, but it usually came from *ad hoc* investigation undertaken by committees of enquiry set up for the purpose—the Committee of Inquiry into Human Fertilisation and Embryology (the Warnock Committee), for instance (22) or by special studies commissioned from, e.g. market researchers or consultants (23). I parted company with the subject in 1987 when we were in the process of doing what I was first involved in nearly 20 years earlier—setting up a new structure under a new Chief Scientist, Professor Francis O'Grady, supported by a new Research Management Division, under a first class Medical Under-Secretary, and a Committee of expert advisors. The objective, yet again, was to relate the programme to the strategic health care priorities (24). Some of the lessons from earlier failures had been learned, perhaps the most important being not to rely too heavily upon a Departmentally-owned and managed resource for this purpose. Research institutions of all kinds abound and some of them, particularly the Nuffield Provincial Hospitals Trust and the King's Fund, have often hit the strategic issue with well-timed and well-managed research studies, or even commissioned surveys of major issues. Enthoven on the purchase of health care is a case in point. Another is the work of the Public Expenditure Policy Unit (PEPU) of the Public Finance Formulation, under Geoffrey Hulme, in connection with 'the review of the NHS'—a series of papers produced by experts, considered in a well-informed wider forum, discussed openly over a short-period and produced as a well-timed prospectus for debate. These are models to be followed.

But, of course, the essential prerequisite for research into health services, their effectiveness, acceptability and cost, is the facility to ask the right questions, to follow them with further questions as necessary, and to feed the findings in openly at the level where relevant decisions are being made—which will not always or even necessarily be the Central Government Department in Whitehall. What is needed for this is a forum for open consideration in a non-polemical environment, free from the parliamentary dogfight. The idea which some of us pursued of an independent Institute for Health has not yet come to fruition. Perhaps its time will soon come. The transfer to it of the Health Services research budget of the Department could be a very good bargain for Ministers; for the health care professions; for the truly competent researchers—and ultimately for the public whose opinions, aspirations, and satisfaction really matter.

# 10

# Does anybody ever listen?

The question is one which, I am sure, has been asked by countless patients and their relatives; by employees professional and lay; by members of the public; by Royal Colleges; and by members of Parliament too. It goes to the heart of the problem of how best to care for the national health. Is anybody or anything truly responsible for hearing (which often means asking) what our society expects or desires for itself in this matter? If so, where and who is it, and to whom accountable?

The questions could hardly be simpler. The answers are infuriatingly complicated. I suspect that is because so many worthy and well-motivated attempts have been made over the years to give positive answers. It is also because uniquely health care is dependant ultimately upon a profession which regards itself as the custodian of the individual patient's interest and can justifiably claim to have been—all too often—the only body able, willing, and committed to fulfil that role.

That professional responsibility is, however, now overlaid with a complex of bodies and authorities which have, could have, or ought to have an interest in providing the positive answer: yes, we heard you and this is what we are doing about it. Without being exhaustive: the several hundred authorities, boards and committees appointed by Secretaries of State to exercise powers of their behalf related to health care; the various formal 'complaint' procedures; the Parliamentary Health Commissioner, and the Select Committee of the House of Commons to which he is answerable; the House of Commons' (and Lords') other Committees; the Members of Parliament; Local Authorities; 'Consumer' organisations, in-

Notes begin on page 85

cluding the special interest lobbies like MENCAP; the media in their self-appointed role; and, of course the scores of Community Health Councils appointed to give voice to the views of the community (25).

All of these are reasonable and generally responsible organs for conveying to the ultimate source of power what the public think or are thought to think about their particular interests. There's the rub: the interest is invariably particular. And predictable in its demand for more resources. I recall no such source ever coming forward with a proposal to stop or reduce an activity and so save money. They will often colour their self-evidently sound proposals for immediate and additional services/improvements with the generalised observation that it will save money in the long run. Maybe. But the books have to be balanced somewhere and at that point more objective analysis is required.

This brings us back to research—or more accurately investigations of the opinions and ideas of the public in the broadest sense. These are often difficult for Government to initiate, especially where, as in most of the 1980s the functioning of the health care system is the substance of not very well-informed party warfare, or embroiled in difficult problems of personnel management. So there is a role for the independent body, be it the King's Fund or the Nuffield Provincial Hospitals Trust, or York University, or PEPU to investigate and report—provided that they are objective and wherever possible point usefully to remedies or actions which are feasible. There has been a fair amount of this in the past, not always heeded, of course. Nevertheless, one hopes that authority, be it Central Government itself or any of the many Authorities responsible for a particular area of health care, will promote more of this kind of investigation. The climate is surely more favourable than it has ever been for finding out what 'customers' (which includes those who pay) think and want before the political commitments are made—and adjusting accordingly. It is always possible that the outcome might be improved.

# 11

# On authority and ownership

And so, after excursions into what will I trust be seen as important and not peripheral matters, we come to the heart of current concern and the most costly part of the health care system, the hospital service. So much has been written already, by way of histories, reports by committees of enquiry and review, evidence to Parliamentary Committees, articles and editorials in learned journals, that a proper reticence and brevity is called for from further contributors. But a few reflections may be in order, starting with authority and ownership.

The key features in this landscape are easily identified:

The Secretary of State* owns virtually everything by way of physical property and equipment in the English hospitals.

The money to run the hospital and community health service is provided annually through the Public Expenditure process, out of Exchequer monies agreed by the Secretary of State with Treasury to be voted by Parliament, and distributed by him to Health Authorities.

The Secretary of State is empowered by Act of Parliament to provide from these resources a service such as he thinks 'reasonable'.

To this end, Regional and District Health Authorities were established, also by authority of Act of Parliament, to deliver hospital and community services throughout the UK.

Following the re-organisation of 1982, the 192 English Districts provide the hospital and community health services through District General Hospitals which for management

* The Secretary of State is a different person of course, in England, Wales, Scotland and Northern Ireland.

Notes begin on page 85

purposes are organised into some 800 units, each now headed by a General Manager. (The 90 Family Practitioner Committees providing the general practitioner service were also part of the District Health Authority's empire from 1974 to 1982, but they were largely ignored by the DHA and made independent from 1982.)

Two kinds of hospital service are, however, still provided directly by the Department of Health: the four Special Hospitals for the detention, care, and treatment of patients whose mental condition by handicap or illness makes them dangerous (Rampton, Broadmoor, Park Lane, and Moss Side); and the Artificial Limb and Appliance Centres providing those facilities to patients disabled by amputation, etc.

The Secretary of State has power to direct the Health Authorities and Boards as he thinks fit on any matter within his responsibility.

The Regional Health Authority has power similarly to direct the Districts.

The Secretary of State's Department is required by Statute to furnish annually accounts of the Health Authorities' expenditure, signed personally by the Permanent Secretary and Accounting Officer, which are subject to audit by the Comptroller and Auditor General (C and A.G) and the National Audit Office.

The Public Accounts Committee examines these accounts and the Accounting Officer on the advice of the C & AG.

The hospitals are free to use and raise their own additional funds from Trust funds and voluntary donations; they can raise other revenues only from statutory charges approved by the Secretary of State. The proceeds from sale of surplus land accrue to the Secretary of State.

Beyond this financial framework the Secretary of State has virtually no power; influence only in certain limited areas; and a few quasi-judicial functions.

The principal influence is, of course, the level and distribution of resources for revenue and capital expenditure by Health Authorities and the size of the centrally determined wage-bill to be met by them.

The content and practice of care provided in hospitals is primarily the responsibility of (a) independent statutory bodies, e.g. the General Medical Council and the Central Nursing Council, as regards professional qualification and conduct; (b) the Royal Colleges as regards the higher levels of specialised training; (c) the several thousand consultants contracted with Regional Health Authorities to provide both services, within some two dozen different specialties, and the supervision and training of junior Doctors below consultant grade.

The University Grants Committee (now the University Funding Council), through its medical Sub-Committee, is responsible for funding through the University system the medical schools of universities located in teaching hospitals. These hospitals provide both undergraduate and postgraduate education and training *and* the services required of a District General Hospital or specialist hospital, for which purpose they are also funded by Regional Health Authorities as Districts. The intake of students into the medical schools necessarily determines the supply of doctors 8 years later; similarly with the intake of students into the schools of nursing, usually co-located, 3–4 years later.

The postgraduate and specialised hospitals in London, which with their related research Institutes constitute the British Postgraduate Medical Federation, are separately funded by the Department of Health, with a substantial input of voluntary funds, especially into the Institutes (26).

Clinical research and development of all kinds is derived from consultant practice in general hospitals as well as from research in the teaching/specialised hospitals and institutes. It is not significantly funded by the Health Authorities (over and above their provision for consultant services). It is funded mainly by the Medical Research Council, the Universities, the various medical research charities and by the UK pharmaceutical companies. The medical equipment companies likewise provide some resources, including equipment, for research and development in their field.

There are, in aggregate, some hundreds of collective bodies engaged in the administration, direction, and delivery of the UK hospital services activities of all kinds—from statutory bodies to expert committees. The numbers of persons having to be appointed to them runs into thousands: many but not all have to be appointed by Ministers; the senior posts require the Prime Minister's approval.

The 'workforce' employed by those bodies in the UK exceeds one million persons, with hundreds of different functions and grades; the terms and conditions of service of most of them are nationally determined by Ministers; for nurses', midwives', doctor's, and dentist's pay is determined on the recommendations of Review Bodies which are normally accepted; the interests of the staff are represented by a miscellany of trade unions or professional bodies most of which have members in fields other than Health Authorities.

This inventory is a long way from being comprehensive; even so a full account of what is entailed in the functioning of each would fill a very substantial volume. At the senior levels in the health care system there will be a good general understanding of this scene and many will know some part of it in great depth. Beyond that I find few who comprehend its breadth and complexity.

Two conclusions can be drawn, each blindingly obvious and, therefore, commonly overlooked. First, it is not possible to demand or enforce change in any one area of this vast array of institutions and processes without affecting other areas, some or all, in some degree. Secondly, it is beyond question not possible to 'manage' the whole of this in any real sense from one central point of authority.

A simple illustration of the two in combination is the cumulative effect on medical education in the undergraduate and postgraduate teaching hospitals of the 'RAWP' process (27). The objective behind RAWP was admirable for the age in which it was formulated, i.e. an era of volume, not cash-limited, financial planning, intended to provide annual increases in real resources for hospital services which could be used progressively to bring less well-provided areas up to a national standard of financial and service provision. (Note the carefully chosen words: financial provision may or may not equate with quality of care.) Given the essential and primary Government objective of the post–IMF era, to reduce inflation and revive the economy by reducing the demands of public expenditure, the RAWP principle had to be applied in a different context. The redistribution had to mean substantial retrenchment from existing plans, rather than only modest growths in the better-placed Districts. Ministers and their senior officials agonised over this during the six years of Public Expenditure Review in which I was involved, trying to strike a fine balance between progress to equalisation and the maintenance of standards in the non-gaining Regions. But none at the centre were involved in the crucial decisions *within* Regions to shift resources away from the 'over-provided' conurbations to the outer areas. And, of course, it was in the inner conurbations that the medical schools were long established. At the same time, provision for medical education was squeezed by the public expenditure/constraints. Nor surprisingly, the pips squeaked. The language of 'cuts in the NHS' was given a powerful voice especially in the London teaching hospitals.

The notes preceding this indicate, I hope, how successive governments' pre-occupation with the framework of Regional and District Health Authorities and their hospitals has led to neglect elsewhere. Even within the hospital field itself, the same point applies. There can, for example, be no more difficult and demanding work in caring for the sick than in the Special Hospitals; and few more sensitive services (or cost-effective, if done well) than the provision of artificial limbs for amputees. The Boynton Report (28) on Rampton and the McColl Report on Artificial Limb and Appliance Centres (29) demonstrate all too clearly how these services, of over-riding importance to the thousands directly affected, deteriorated because they had become marginal to the main business of Government.

Others better qualified than I could give further examples no doubt. For my present purposes it is perhaps sufficient to point to the lessons which need to be learned—that authority cannot be exercised where one's writ does not run, i.e. where the ownership belongs to other bodies or institutions; that attempting too much will have the inescapable consequence of some matters being done badly; and that the first duty of the centre is to see the whole and understand how it all relates. The burden of ultimate responsibility for health services and their institutions will, of course, remain with the central Department of State in some degree under any conceivable programme of 'modernisation', especially while the most costly services of all are financed mainly and directly by the Exchequer. But the centre cannot manage what it does not truly own, and/or cannot grasp because of its size, and complexity. Some process of, and mechanism for delegation and accountability, will therefore be essential. But before addressing that, a brief return to the myths and illusions of Chapter 3.

# 12

# The hidden agenda

Government Departments have long been thought to cherish and promote their own policies, irrespective of the passing thoughts of Ministerial tenants. The Foreign and Commonwealth Office 'is pro-EEC and pro-Arab'; the Department of Transport 'is all for roads'; the Department of Industry 'for regional development'; the Treasury 'against public expenditure' and DoE 'in favour of Local Government per se'. These may be caricatures. But the hidden agenda can be a reality, though hard to pin down, and the Department of Health was a case in point.

It was for example, and for all I know still is, in the minds of some engaged in the health business at central Government level, that it would be better managed if hospitals could be 'returned' to Local Authorities (30). Failing that, they might be combined with social services under one even larger umbrella, of air-ship dimensions. Another example: the Social Security provision through Supplementary Benefit for residential accommodation for the elderly and the handicapped having been allowed to expand as a demand-led benefit, should be switched to the HCHS Vote and re-directed to the general provision of services to the elderly, etc., under the control of Health Authorities. These ideas were never to be found written down but they have a life of their own and break surface sooner or later (31).

They are not perceived only within the Department. They are at least suspected by interests outside. It is not surprising to anyone sensitive to these possibilities that the BMA's CCHMS* should be prepared to die in a ditch to keep consultants' contracts at Regional level, rather than have them made with Districts, which stand so near to Local Govern-

---

* Central Committee for Hospital Medical Services.

Notes begin on page 86

ment. Another example was the sensitivity of the doctors in general practice to the idea of a restricted list of prescribable medicines in certain generic categories: lying behind that sensitivity was the conviction of the doctors that the ultimate Departmental goal is compulsory generic substitution, another hidden agenda candidate.

One such idea that was very audible when I returned to the Department in 1981 was that—perhaps en route to Local Government—the about-to-be-constituted District Health Authorities should be their own masters. Once endowed with their 'crock of gold', it would be for them to spend it without interference or meddling by Regional Health Authorities or the Department. The RHAs could be abolished, thus adding to the quango-cull. The Department could be slimmed down even more. All would be well. This was a grand idea that would have met one of the major requirements for less-costly-to-administer health services—the disengagement of Ministers and Parliament from the minutiae of it. Unfortunately, it was an illusion because it ran headlong into the principle of accountability to Parliament for expenditure of public funds.

# 13

# Delegation and accountability

In July 1981 the Public Accounts Committee published its
17th report of that session on 'Financial control and accountability in the NHS' which dealt directly with the issue of
accountability to Parliament for the large sums appropriated to
Health Authorities. The Committee clashed directly with the
idea of devolving all responsibility for that expenditure on the
individual Health Authority, and recorded their judgement in
two seminal paragraphs:

'The PAC of Session 1976–77 rejected the concept of
separate votes for individual Health Authorities, which they
thought would lead to fragmentation of financial control in
the health service. We endorse their view and note that the
Regional Chairmen agreed with the Government's rejec-
tion of the Royal Commission's proposal that Regional
Health Authorities should become directly accountable to
Parliament.'

'On the basis of these (i.e. the C&A.G.'s) Reports, the
three Accounting Officers of the Health Departments give
evidence to us for the whole of the NHS expenditure. In
our view the impending NHS re-organisation will accentu-
ate their difficulty and particularly that of the DHSS
Accounting Officer in reconciling that accountability with
the greater delegation of day-to-day management decisions
to the Health Authorities.'

The issue was not new. It had lain unresolved since the
'Grey Book' was published in 1972, following the McKinsey-
based review which led to the 1974 re-organisation. The
principle was stated then that delegation must be matched by
accountability. But no clear prescription was given as to how
this was to be achieved, especially in a management structure

Notes begin on page 86

which intentionally fragmented overall responsibility between the members of multi-disciplinary teams. By 1981 little progress had been made on this and, as the PAC perceived, the thrust seemed to be in the opposite direction: hands off.

This was not only seen by the PAC as an abdication, and therefore unacceptable—a view the Treasury was bound to share. It was of no avail against remorseless pressure from the Parliamentary constituencies and lobbies for more and greater Ministerial involvement. And it took no account of the fact that the existing central responsibility for pay and conditions of service of Health Authority personnel made it inevitable that Ministers and the Department would get deeply involved, as they had been in the 1978–79 'winter of discontent', as counter-inflationary policies began to bite again.

The way out of this wrangle was evolved, in late 1981, in discussions I had with the Comptroller and Auditor-General (Sir Gordon Downey), the Principal Finance Officer (Geoffrey Hulme), the Under Secretary in charge of the Regional Liaison Division (Brian Rayner), the two Junior Ministers Sir Gerard Vaughan and Sir Geoffrey Finsberg, and the new Secretary of State Norman Fowler. The idea was simple: the Department would each year review with each RHA Chairman and his principal officers the progress achieved by the RHA towards objectives agreed with Ministers for the past year, and reach agreement on performance targets for the year ahead. The RHA Chairman supported it and the policy was announced by the Secretary of State in January 1982 (32). It began to be implemented that year and was extended afterwards to reviews of the performance of DHAs, SHAs and, later, FPCs when they became established in a direct line of accountability to the Secretary of State. This was the first of three major steps in a radical revision of the management of the hospital service. The precise details of a review system are unimportant. They have changed and will change again but I hope that the principle will stand: he who regularly receives the taxpayer's money has an obligation regularly to demonstrate that it is being spent to good purpose, with betterment of performance in terms of value for money and objectives achieved.

The second and related step was the definition, first achieved in a pilot project in the Northern Regional Health Authority in 1982, of performance indicators which would make possible comparative analysis of Districts' performance. This was initially crude, and laughably cumbersome in terms of the volume of paper generated. Information technology has solved the paper problem. A greater obstacle was the continuing resistance to the idea of comparative evaluation, largely out of fears that it would be used in a mechanical and simplistic way. These fears will remain, and each refinement and development will refuel them. But the tide will not turn (33). The pressures on public expenditure and the demand for better performance in using it will continue inexorably. If it ever happens that alternative systems of finance should evolve, one can confidently predict that the new paymasters will be no less rigorous.

The third step was the result of a different but concurrent development: the industrial dispute of 1982, which brings us to the difficult field of industrial relations in health care.

# 14

# Employers, employees
# and contractors

Aspiring consultants in personnel management might as a test of ingenuity, be asked to construct a model which meets the following specification:

A hospital service for consultation and treatment will be provided by 200+ different employing authorities.

The most senior clinical posts in the hospitals, and the highest paid, will be filled by independent contractors whose contracts will be not with the authority providing the service but a Regional Health Authority.

The contractors will have authority to determine the demand for in-patient services; will be free to work part-time (up to 10 per cent of their time) on private work nominally unconnected with the hospital service; will have security of tenure save for proven misbehaviour until retirement age; and will receive higher pay for meritorious work on the judgement of the profession without reference to the hospital authority.

Other posts will be filled by employees of the Authority.

Clinicians in grades below consultants will be employed on short-term contracts. All other employees will be permanently employed.

Permanent employees will have, by statute, the status of Crown Servants; will not be civil servants as such but will have inherited a grading and pay structure aligned originally with the Civil Service; will have security of tenure in their *grade* and, at the more senior levels, also in the *posts* to which they are appointed.

The terms and conditions of service of employees will be determined subject to the approval of Ministers, on a national basis of negotiation in joint (Whitley) Committees of representatives of employing authorities and representatives of the trade unions to which the employees belong.

The resultant wage and salary bill of both employees and contractors will normally be met by the Hospital Authorities out of their predetermined budgets.

Employees in the professions of nursing, midwifery, medicine, and dentistry will have their pay determined by independent Review Bodies appointed by the Prime Minister.

Senior posts in all Authorities will be filled by open competition; the normal pathway to these posts will entail transfer from one Authority to another; there will be no central oversight of these transfers, and no uniform standards of qualification to the higher posts.

There will be no compulsory, formal, and centrally supervised training for promotion and no system of career planning and management for the most able.

The work-force to be accommodated in this framework will comprise approximately one million people in 20 or so different professional disciplines or administrative and other skills; it will be represented by nearly 20 registered trade unions or other bodies.

One could go on. The end result of this amalgam is a uniquely complex structure which seems to combine the inherited rigidities of a Civil Service grading system, but without its central authority, with the fragmented responsibilities of the Local Government system. It is now overlaid for the main professional grades (and, because nurses are included, for half the work-force) by the inflexibilities of Pay Review Body System. No sane person would set about creating anew a labour-intensive massive service with this degree of complexity in the personnel function. But here it is; with a life of its own and, seemingly, an indefinite future ahead of it.

The core of the problem lies in the fact that we have managed to avoid for decades resolving the question whether this is a single, disciplined, work-force characterised by a sense of loyalty and commitment to one service, or whether it is an essentially local payroll subject like local government and education in particular, to central governments' constraints. It is hardly surprising that there are conflicts of loyalty, made the more inevitable since most of the work-force directly serving patients has a professional ethic which puts first the interest of the patient not the interest of the employer.

Even more significant is the fact that because over half the work-force is in self-regulating professions, Central Government—although the ultimate employer in the sense that it foots the bill—has no real weapons with which to monitor and control performance. There has been no Inspectorate of the quality of care, and only in recent years a modest form of 'peer review' by the Hospital Advisory Service. The conventional audit process cannot bite on the content of the service provided; and the remit of the Health Commissioner stops short of any clinical complaint.

There are, of course, good and compelling reasons why the hospital structure has evolved in this way over several decades. There are most certainly no simple or speedy routes to a better system or even a substantial improvement in the performance of the present system. An employee-contractor work-force of some million individuals is plainly not manageable in any real sense from a single point of power in Whitehall. It will be in the interests of all concerned—from Ministers to porters, from the highest ranking clinician to the patient and the taxpayer —if a real and manageable employer/employee relationship could be evolved. It is happening slowly. The first steps emerged from the industrial dispute of 1982.

# 15

# A strike in the NHS hospitals

The NHS dispute of 1982 will, I believe, be of lasting significance in this context. It was due to a concerted attempt by the 13 unions represented in the TUC Health Services Committee to achieve a uniform flat-rate pay settlement for all NHS employees of 12 per cent from 1 April 1982, the uniform starting date having already been conceded. The 12 per cent was intended to sustain the substantial increases made by the Clegg Commission on Comparability which was devised in the aftermath of 'the winer of discontent' 1978–79. It was, however, essential for good government that the threat of a re-run of 1978–79 be faced down. It was essential for the defeat of inflation that a 'norm' of 12 per cent be defeated. And it was essential for good management that the concept of a uniform flat-rate increase for all, irrespective of demand, skill, performance, and ability to pay, be overturned. This meant accepting what was widely seen as unacceptable: holding out against trade union pressure through 'industrial action', even though services began to be substantially affected.

What followed is history. The biggest ever UK industrial dispute, until Mr Scargill and the NUM went one better, was endured. A much more modest and differential settlement providing more for nurses was established, with a Pay Review Body for Nurses and Midwives to be introduced the following year. More importantly perhaps, the RCN established the principle which they have managed to sustain since, that their members constitute a profession which does not take strike action.

The dispute began in March and ended in December 1982. The small group of Ministers and senior officials involved led

Notes begin on page 87

a weary and lonely life during this time: the expectation in the hospital service and in the professions, in the media and in Parliament was that, of course, we should compromise so that this dreadful dispute could be resolved. Allies were few. The trade unions led by the late Albert Spanswick (34), a good and gentle man, were similarly harrassed: it was evidently thought to be obvious by their members that an unpopular Government would give way, as in 1979, if enough pressure were applied. The concurrent Falklands conflict, with all its political controversy, was encouraging to this point of view and unsettling to Government. In the background there was an even more important factor: the seemingly endless expansion in the size of the hospital workforce, which was bound to make it that much harder to constrain public expenditure, so as to defeat inflation and release resources for economic recovery.

All these elements led to the conclusion that we could not go on with the management of the Health Authorities workforce as we had been—a conclusion shared by Albert Spanswick and Peter Jacques (34), with whom we always maintained good relations at all times. It was in many talks with them that the idea evolved of an enquiry into NHS manpower and management when the dispute was settled. So the seeds were sown which produced eventually the Review of NHS Management by Sir Roy Griffiths, Sir Brian Bailey, Michael Bett, and James Blyth.

# 16

# A new centre, a new style of management?

The two main conclusions of the Management Review were that consensus management in the hospitals and their Authorities be replaced by general management* and that the new style of management be led and directed from the centre by a NHS Management Board with professional members in all relevant disciplines, including especially personnel management. There were nearly 20 more proposals but all rested on these two (35). Taken together with the establishment of 'accountability review'; i.e. a review by the next higher level of authority of the year's performance measured against agreed objectives, and with the development of performance indicators in a more sensitive and accessible form, the Griffiths recommendations were intended to establish a more rational framework for the relationship between Ministers and their Departments on the one hand and the Health Authorities on the other.

It was nearly a disaster. The proposals were broadly accepted by the Government and the first step, the establishment of a NHS Supervisory Board chaired by the Secretary of State, was announced concurrently with the publication of the Report in October 1983. Urgent consultation with the professions was set in train, the House of Commons Social Services Committee joined in, draft circulars were prepared and the introduction of General Management was begun in April 1984. Meanwhile Mr Victor Paige was asked to chair the Management Board and set about this task with vigour and

---

* i.e a single officer personally responsible, in consultation as necessary with other relevant disciplines, for the efficient despatch of all business and of the services provided by the authority to whom he was accountable.

Notes begin on page 87

imagination, assembling an impressive team of expertise from the private sector to work alongside high quality people from the Department, including the Chief Medical Officer and Chief Nursing Officer (36). But running below the surface were two conflicting currents. One was the widely held belief, especially among the hospital service Administrators and Health Authority Chairmen, that this was the beginning of a long-awaited freedom from interference from Government: the independent body to manage the NHS on its own (the NHS Management Board) was to be realised at last. The other was the belief of Ministers and some officials that this was a body set up primarily to introduce into the management of the hospitals a competence, energy, and discipline which had been manifestly lacking—freedom for Health Authorities to cut loose and pursue their own paths at the taxpayer's expense was the last thing in any of our minds.

The unrealisable expectations of the hospital service chiefs were in part the consequence of failing to read the Griffiths' Report. It was quite clear that this was, as it could only be, an administrative reform within the existing statutory framework and that all powers remained as they were. The authority behind the new management process and the new structures was the Secretary of State's, the finance was provided by Parliamentary Vote, and accountability was to be more, not less rigorously imposed. But, of course, the main source of the unrealisable expectation was our old friend, the grand illusion that somehow a mechanism could be and had been devised under which Government would hand over £15b plus per annum of Exchequer Funds to be spent at discretion by independent authorities with Ministers and their officials kept at arms length.

The conflict of ideas was slowly and painfully resolved. But, fortunately, this was not before Victor Paige and his colleagues had pretty well established what some of us had pinned our hopes on, that it was both possible and advantageous from every point of view to establish a 'centre' for the hospital service; dependent (of course) on the authority of Ministers but, given their backing, able to generate enthusiasm and new ideas for the betterment of the service. The new ideas began to emerge especially in the personnel field when Mr Len Peach, recruited from IBM as Personnel Director, began the process of radically reforming the pay structure by establishing a system of higher but performance-related pay starting with the general managers. This was not only designed and promulgated in a remarkably short time—much quicker, and with a much better scheme, than happened in the Civil Service—but was meticulously processed through the Ministerial and official machinery of government and taken deftly through the Parliamentary minefield by Norman Fowler with—as usual—a misleading low profile. It was, ironically, on the threshold of this major advance that Victor Paige felt obliged to resign in June 1986, not recognising perhaps how much had been achieved under his chairmanship in a short time. My inability to persuade him not to remains a dismal memory.

The issues arising from this episode are of continuing significance and not only for the administration and management of the health care system as a whole. By comparison with what could have been done by Chief Executive in a commercial environment it may have appeared and evidently was perceived as too little. But Government never was and never will be like commercial business. The process of trying to bring some of the virtues of the business approach into central functions relating to the hospital service was, and will continue to be, demanding and fretful. Inevitably tensions will arise between, on the one hand, Ministers (and those officials supporting them) who must always be accountable to Parliament, and on the other officials (irrespective of their nomenclature) who had been charged by those same Ministers with the task of achieving an efficient delivery of services within prescribed policies and pre-determined resources.

After Victor Paige's resignation much thought was given at the highest levels as to the best way of handling the next stage in the development of the NHS Management Board. In what I saw as a necessarily interim move, which for the time being by-passed the potential conflicts with Ministers, it was decided that the Minister of State for Health should take on the chairmanship and Mr Len Peach be appointed as Chief Executive.

Some of us were clear that this was an interim solution pending more fundamental thinking about the future of the NHS on other grounds (see p. 1) but it had two obvious merits. First, it reflected an agreed view that immediate past frustrations had not undermined the case for a management board at the centre, not as a body to manage in a line-manager sense but to conduct efficiently those functions relating to the management of the Health Authorities which had perforce to be done in the central department. Secondly, it secured in the lead official role as Chief Executive, in Len Peach, someone with a flair for both personnel management and multi-disciplinary working which was crucially important.

On a wider front, the NHS Management Board story is relevant to—and was reflected in the thinking of—the Prime Minister's Efficiency Unit Report on 'The Next Steps'. It is no accident that they key Annex to that Report (Annex A: Accountability to Ministers and Parliament on operational matters) refers to the NHS Management Board and the Regional and District Health Authorities in its delphic appraisal of the relationship between executive 'agencies', Ministers *and Parliament*. The key to the future development of our health care system—its scope, structure, finance, and functioning in every respect, not just the hospital service—lies in my view in the definition of the role of Parliament.

# 17

# Parliament: the actor-manager on a crowded stage

A roll-call of those I have mentioned so far as having a role in our health care system would be long. Most of them, however, even the bit-players, have a fairly specific role assigned to them, sometimes by Parliament itself in statute-law, sometimes by Ministers, sometimes by circumstances. But Parliament? The legislative process seems to oscillate between the political punch-up, which takes up much media time or space, and the tedium of grinding through the over-elaborate detail in legislative proposals, the amendment of which is as likely to be eccentric as useful. There is too much legislation anyway and in a better-ordered world there would certainly be much less need to embody in statute law and statutory instruments so much of the fine detail of a health care system.

Running in continuous performance, with the not-too-frequent general debate as an interlude, is the steady flow of Parliamentary Questions, with the monthly parade of Ministers to answer orally the first 50 or so, leaving the remainder to be included among the mass of other 'written' answers. Then there are the special performances when the Secretary of State and his colleagues have to make a statement on some matter of importance. Behind the public scenes, a stream of activity goes on as MPs take up with Ministers their constituency cases or lobbies or issues. This volume of PQs, MP letters, and meetings is vast, and costly to service. The cost is, of course, the necessary price of democracy; and the driving force behind it—the individual's right to seek redress of grievance or even information through his representative in Parliament—is part of the power of Parliament which will never allow an Exchequer-funded system to break free of its control. (Our old

Notes begin on page 89

friend the grand illusion would, of course, hope otherwise). But unavoidable though it is, this spate of words seems in large degree marginal to what ought to be the central interest of Parliament in the national health.

We come nearer to that interest in the work of the Select Committees. The Permanent Secretary has a special relationship with one: The Public Accounts Committee. That relationship can be and in my experience was a powerful reinforcement of the Permanent Secretary's authority and an even more powerful incentive for him or her to take very seriously his obligations to ensure that publicly-financed programmes of expenditure are managed with integrity and efficiency. When the PAC 'blew the whistle' in 1981 they were, in effect, saying to the Accounting Officer that the hands-off policy was delegation without accountability and incompatible with his statutory obligations. I believe they were right. The PAC's formal remit is directed to the financial dimension; their investigations must start from the certified accounts and the reports of the National audit Office thereon. But their proper interest in value-for-money, which is now much more recognised, enables them to adopt a broad approach and review wide areas of policy. An example is their successive investigations of the effectiveness of expenditure on the family practitioner services—optical, dental and pharmaceutical—and on prevention of ill-health (37).

They are able to do this because they have the support of a public servant of the highest rank (the Comptroller and Auditor General), heading an office (the National Audit Office—NAO) of able and qualified people *with continuous access to the Department's files by NAO officers who are outstationed in each Department.* The resultant relationship between the Secretary of State's officials and the C&AG's officers is anything but cosy: a mutual admiration society it is not. Some of the most fractious dog fights in my experience occurred in this quarter. The crucial element which gives the Committee its strength, however, is that the C&AG's reports must be agreed with the Department as to the facts; and, as to the judgements, must be agreed in terms which record disagreements and the reason for them. The Committee is, therefore, well placed to take on the issues in a considered way. It would be absurd to describe one's appearances before the PAC as pleasurable. They are recorded both for the written record and for radio, so that one is liable to hear one's convoluted efforts to explain the inexplicable high-lighted in one of the BBC's Parliamentary programmes. And they are always interlocutory: questions have to be answered. But within that framework relevant and informative discussion can take place.

The Permanent Secretary also has a special, though different, relationship with the Select Committee on the Parliamentary Commissioner and Health Commissioner. This is because the Ombudsman will always reach his judgement on a complaint on the basis of investigations carried out in the relevant area by his own officers (cf. the C&AG) *and* of a response by '*the principal officer*', i.e. the Permanent Secretary of the Department concerned. The principal officer's responsibility is taken very seriously: one was obliged to examine all the documents oneself and write personally to the Commissioner giving an explanation of events and either a defence or an admission of culpability. A similar obligation rests upon the principal officers of Health Authorities and FPCs. The Health Commissioner's judgements, and a summary record of the cases he dealt with during the year, are then considered by the Select Committee and the Permanent Secretary, among others, is called to give evidence. This annual appearance was much less confrontational than the PAC appearances and in the result tended more towards discussion of problems with, of course, the Committee properly wanting to know what the Department was doing about them.

The Health Commissioner for most of my time as Permanent Secretary was Sir Cecil Clothier and he has recorded his reflections as my predecessor in his Rock Carling Lecture. His work *The Patient's Dilemma* makes very clear the insight into the quality of, or lack of, care which the Health Commissioner acquires. It gives too little credit, however, to the pressure for betterment which his role applies to the health care system (38). The widespread dissemination through the system of his 'epitomes' has, as was reported back to us, a considerable impact on the awareness of staff in all disciplines of the patient's view of their attitudes. Less well known, but just as important, is the pressure of the Health Commissioner and the Select Committee for the clinical complaints procedure (39) to be made to work effectively.

These two Select Committees operate to very considerable effect because they are under-pinned by their own dedicated staff with the numbers, skills, and authority to acquire their evidence for them. The third Select Committee which bears on our interest, the Social Services Committee, lacks that resource. It is supported by officers of the House of Commons as its secretariat but relies for its evidence on material supplied to it on those subjects which the Committee itself elects to pursue. There is no special relationship with the Permanent Secretary or any other officer of the Department—Ministers and/or officials submit material and are invited to appear before the Committee and 'give evidence', sometimes at considerable length. The Committee's reports are in a different category from the PAC reports, with the PAC regularly following up progress on matters it has raised. The Social Services Committee reports take broader themes—the services for the care of children, or the Report on NHS Management for example. And they are in the nature of the case likely to be of a more political nature, i.e. addressing issues of policy which require a political response rather than investigating the operations of services in this field (40).

I was long ago persuaded that the Parliamentary function would be better served by the institution of Select Committees of the kind now in being, broadly covering the major fields of Government responsibility. They are not yet an unqualified success but will I trust develop further. This development will, however, if it is to be worthwhile and effective, require that the Departmental Select Committees have resources for their own investigation and, equally important, that the Department's resources are available to meet their requirements. An effective Parliament does not come cheap, either in its own parish or in the departments of Government. At the moment the public, Parliament, the taxpayer, and those working in the health care system at all levels are not getting a very good bargain: to many routine and trivial questions, letters, and political encounters; too much that could and should be taken up locally raised to the national level; and too little consideration of issues of national interest, worthy of Parliament.

The Parliamentary role functioning well was I think visible in the process of legislation on mental health leading to the setting up of the Mental Health Commission in the 1983 Act. This employed the new and rare procedure of a Parliamentary Committee taking evidence before the passage of the Bill at 'pre-legislative hearings'. The subject matter was, of couse, by then widely recognised as of great sensitivity in regard to the civil liberties of mentally ill or handicapped patients, their treatment and confinement where appropriate, and the safety of the public. But it is not unique; nor do these kind of issues arise only infrequently in Parliamentary consideration: the sexual and other abuse of children; *in vitro* fertilisation and related research; the control of infection by HIV and the spread of AIDS, are recent examples where the Parliamentary process has to be engaged, sooner or later. Parliament deserves to be better equipped (though there is, of course, another more cynical view which would argue that if the Parliamentary Select Committee remains at its present level of effectiveness it will be that much easier for the executive to ignore or override it). And it should be able to focus on matters central to health care but now commonly neglected. For present purposes let the record speak for itself. I enquired how frequently had Parliament debated any of the annual reports of the Government's Chief Medical Officer. These reports have been produced in a virtually unbroken series for over a century. They are carefully prepared to give an authoritative appraisal of the state of the public health in general and with particular reference to matters of immediate or imminent importance or difficulty. So far as we could ascertain, the answer is never.

# 18

# About money and value, price and payment

These simple words take us into an area of gross muddle and confusion. To begin with money, there are only six possible sources of finance for the purchase of health care:

Central Government's Exchequer funds, paid for by the general body of taxpayers;

Local Government funds, paid for by rate-payers today and community-charge payers shortly, with additional funds from the Exchequer;

'national', i.e. State-run, schemes of health or social insurance to which all or most of the adult population are or were contributors;

'private' schemes of health insurance to which individuals and groups of employees or members contribute, with or without employer or state subsidy, e.g. by tax concessions;

charitable funds in great variety, ranging from well-endowed national trusts and fund-raising bodies to local enterprises to meet a particular need or provide a particular service;

the individual's own resources.

Each of these has been tapped continuously in the UK since 1911, and still is. What happens over the years, of course, is that the proportional input from each changes as circumstances change. The biggest single shift was from the last to the first, but it has not remained constant, nor should it. There is no self-evidently right and permanent relationship between these sources. Unfortunately, what ought to be an informed pragmatic judgement about the best mix at any particular time

Notes begin on page 90

is clouded by dogma, which characterises a source as either acceptable or anathema politically. The result has been that the mix has been exclusively determined at the level of national government. This inhibits initiative at all levels. The assumption that choice about resourcing is a matter only for central government means that government alone is seen as the scapegoat for all inadequacies.

There have been various attempts inside central Government, and without, to find a better mix of resources for a national health care system than we have now. 'Better' means (a) reducing the degree of dependance on central Government finance and (b) enhancing the status of the patients by endowing them with, in effect, their own resources which the provider will tap in return for services rendered. So far none has materialised. The right approach in my view, is clear: every health care Authority will need an under-pinning grant from Central Government in one form or another in return for which it will undertake to provide health services, but it would then be free and expected to raise such other resources, by such means, as it thought appropriate to provide the best possible service in the field for which it has responsibility. The Authority could be elected or appointed (a combination of both confuses accountability). All manner of guiding principles and practices would be wrapped round it, no doubt, the more so if Parliament and Ministers continue their bad habits. But it would have what is now missing, the incentive and freedom to maximise the resources available to provide the best possible service.

The 'best possible'—a question-begging phrase which brings us to value, easily the most difficult aspect of health care management, and health care policy; sadly neglected by Parliament, Ministers, and the whole administrative hierarchy. The subject bristles with difficulty. Perfect health of mind and body? Amelioration of pain and disability in default of prevention or cure? Prevention of premature death? Prevention of disabled life? Here is a morass of moral and conceptual problems through which the right path is hard indeed to find. So, in the jargon of econometrics, we have for practical purposes, to concentrate on 'intermediate outputs'.

But how inadequate some of these are, especially when seized upon to attack or defend a party political record. Waiting list sizes and durations; beds/wards/units/hospitals opened or closed or suspended; treatments given or not given in every specialty of medicine; immunisation take-up—the catalogue of intermediate outputs is vast and bewildering and, like the performance indicators already referred to (33), serves only to prompt further and too-often unanswerable questions.

Nevertheless, public and well-informed consideration of these issues is highly desirable and, at present, sadly lacking save in a few specialised precincts like the Departments of universities studying health economics and a few specialists inside Government Departments. Addressing the question of the ultimate goals of health care is going to be uncomfortable for politicians and dangerous for those in the health care profession unless it is addressed with great sensitivity and honesty. It requires a better debating forum than the House of Commons alone (41).

The debate cannot avoid taking account of price, i.e. what is the real cost of any clinical episode or process *in its entirety*: the health centre, and general practitioner, out-patient and in-patient services; specialist services; pharmaceutical services; and community services; and not forgetting the cost of servicing and maintaining the capital investment. We are chasing a moon-beam if we believe that the vast resources devoted to health care can be better and well-managed if it is impossible to link activity with its cost. But, one can foresee the risk of an elaborate costing process being developed with a fatal flaw in it. If pricing is intended to serve 'efficient management' only by confronting spenders with the theoretical consequences of their actions, the process will eventually fall into disuse or create dissatisfaction. The only good reason for pricing anything is so that it can be paid for, preferably by a 'customer' or 'consumer' or 'patient' who has the choice of going elsewhere. If the price exists only as a notional charge on another employee or unit in the same organisation and never reaches a real customer, its life expectancy will be short. One can easily foresee the Management Services or Consultancy report which (taking a leaf out of Marks and Spencer's good-housekeeping onslaught on paper) demonstrates how much paper and IT input and output could be saved by simplifying, aggregating, standardising, and eventually eliminating the internal pricing process.

Which brings us to payment, i.e. customers or patients being asked to pay. This is where I came in: the bogus row over prescription charges and the muddled thinking that has continued ever since. The issue of charging patients has always been argued politically as an issue of principle. It deserves to be addressed as a practical question: whether a charge can reasonably be levied and generally afforded (exceptions of course for those who cannot afford the charge) so as first, to encourage economical use of resources, both from those whose treatment results in a charge on their patients, and from the patients too; and secondly to generate additional resources.

There is, of course, a lot of cash changing hands in the system now. Patients (or their agents) pay general practitioners for examinations and prescriptions for particular services; hospitals have, almost universally, a cash-based supplement to the hotel services in the shape of the ward trolley services and shops. And the 'hotel charge', which was originally contemplated as a proper element in the hospital services financing system (42), has been in existence since 1948 in a characteristically distorted form, by abatement of Social Security benefits for long-stay patients to take account of 'home-saving'. There cannot be a moral or serious objection to seeking a direct payment for services rendered in a national health care system from an adult literate population which is already willing to pay for what it wants by way of services in immense variety: an annual subscription to the AA, a fee for a renewable passport, and a renewable vehicle licence; an annual fee for a broadcasting receiver licence; annual subscriptions by the million to a miscellany of voluntary and charitable activities; a weekly pools premium; the list is endless. I can see no reason why the citizen should not renew his membership of the national health care system by a premium payment of £20 to the local FPC or Health Authority (or to the NHS Central Register in Southport, of whose existence he will not even be aware, of course). The extra resources would be useful even if the Treasury took a slice, as it should. But, even more important, it would substantially enhance the citizen's sense of ownership and responsibility as taxation does not; and even more important it would enhance the patient's value in the eyes of the providers.

# 19

# In perspective

Many of these reflections surfaced in my mind when I had not only ceased to have any responsibility for health matters but was in Southern Africa. That distance, of time and space, put into perspective our incessant fiddling with our national health institutions and our complacency about their virtues. These notes from Southern Africa may explain why.

*January 1988.* Visited the polio clinic and rehabilitation unit run by a voluntary consortium in Lilongwe, Malawi. A recent epidemic of polio has left many disabled survivors. They are brought in for treatment by car or carried, or as best they may. The young children are accompanied by one parent or relative who will sleep under the bed during in-patiency. The rehabilitation unit is the only source of invalid aids, which are made on the spot: hand and knee pads for 'walking' made out of old tyres cut up to an appropriate shape. Porgy would recognise his trolley, which has to be pushed by hand using the hand-pads. Invalid tricycles are the 'Rolls-Royces' of appliances provided. They are made by cannibalising old bicycles, the frame turned upside down so that the crank can be hand driven. Oxfam sent two containers of wrecked bicycles: a great asset.

*May 1988.* Visited the Howard Institute hospital, 80 km north of Harare, Zimbabwe. A small district hospital run by the Salvation Army and serving an area of 600 square km. A school of nursing is attached, but the output of trained nurses has been interrupted by the extension of training to three years. There is talk of extending nurse training up to degree standard; such is the preoccupation learned from Western Europe and the USA with academic qualifications. The Lt Col surgeon in charge, from the United States and with decades of Third World experience, talks of the community role of the hospital. There is no transportation to it so the field work is crucial. He is concerned about the young children because they are ill mainly from the preventable diseases of children, but pleased that immunisation against measles is now reaching about 70 per cent of the very young, better than parts of the UK.

*May 1988.* Visited the Kamuzu Central Hospital in Lilongwe, with two of its three consultants (both British, one a paediatrician with 16 years experience there; the third Danish). A 350-bed hospital given by Denmark as a standard Scandinavian design hospital. Four floors, so lifts are a heavy running cost—the site is large enough to have housed a bungalow building. The building is fully and extensively glazed—very hot inside (in the 'cold' season). Aid is not always given with imagination. Another donor is providing an Intensive Care Unit—there will not be trained nurses to service it, nor the number of cases to justify it. In any case, many patients will die for want of much more basic medicine. The hospital is more than full—about 800 patients, sleeping in, under and beside the beds. But clean. The medical staff are Malawian Clinical Officers, i.e. one year academic study, two–three years apprenticeship in a hospital and then learning by experience. Very highly spoken of by the UK consultants ('better than your average Registrar in a DGH') and the local white expatriates. All patients routinely tested for HIV—60 per cent positive. Promiscuity and venereal disease are rife and provide the environment for transmission of HIV heterosexually: homosexuality is not a significant factor. The Paediatric Department plunges into one of Dante's circles. It is crammed-full of babies and mothers, each packed so tight that the consultant said he had had to discharge those near the door most likely to survive in order to get to the others. One in three of all Malawi children dies before age 5. One in four of those admitted dies, one recovers, two are taken away before treatment is effected because the mothers/fathers can no longer stay away from their settlement land; their outcome is unknown. Babies too are routinely tested for HIV—the positives are doubling every 6–8 months and have reached 5 per cent. The prognosis is obscure and it is possible that these will not turn into AIDS cases. The consultant says that the population is expected to grow from 9m to 13m by

2000 but on present form there may be 2m deaths from AIDS by then.

All peoples have their problems; some, perhaps, are more urgent. But apart from pricking our consciences, it is possible that the Third World may have lessons for us. The Princess Royal, as President of Save the Children Fund, had pointed out while I was still in the Department that the support for mothers and young children which SCF were providing for villagers in their African projects was better than the help our system provided for mothers and young children, especially in the ethnic minorities, in some of our urban deserts. A degree of modesty about our achievements would become us all.

# 20
# Of hazards, headwinds and guiding lights

This chapter is itself a hazard. I lay no claim to knowing better answers to the conundrums than any of those currently engaged in the search. What follows are reflections derived from past experience reviewed from a distance. Much of it can be deduced from the little essays that have gone before.

The gravest hazard of all would be to continue, as we have for so long, to embody our health care system in a structure of Authorities without a truly defined role and which, in consequence, allows power to be exercised without true responsibility and accountability or a clear sense of purpose. Regional Health Authorities, District Health Authorities, Special Health Authorities, Community Health Councils, Family Practitioner Committees, Representative and Consultative Committees—what exactly is the role of each and for what and by whom should it be called to account—if at all? Addressing those questions raises, of course, the consequential: how should these Authorities, etc be constructed? Why, for example, are Local Authorities formally represented on a District Health Authority? Was it only to appease them in the 1974 reconstruction when the long-established and valuable function of the Medical Officer of Health was taken away, and very largely lost sight of in the submerged role of the community physician? Or was it secure integration, in community care, of the social services with the hospital services and family practitioner services—in which case it has been a failure made the more certain by the growth of a privately-financed and managed residential care system and the withdrawal of the family practitioner services from the remit of the District Health Authorities. The Management Review of 1983 asked a related question about the respective roles of officers and members of Health Authorities—who is respon-

sible for what as between Chairman, members and officers?
We had made no progress in finding an answer, indeed we had
not begun to try, when I left in 1987, but it is second to the
more fundamental question—what are the Authorities and
their members there for at all; and are they needed?

There are three aspects of the present structure which point
up the need for change. First, the dreary burden of appointing
and reappointing hundreds of worthy people, usually in some
kind of representative capacity to sit as members or chairmen
of these bodies: the burden of Ministerial patronage. On a
change of government as in 1979 those processes take on,
inevitably, a further element of party political patronage as
services of various kinds are rewarded at no great cost. As time
passes, and as the accountability process begins to bite,
personal capacity rather than affiliation weighs more heavily,
which is all to the good. But the question remains: why are
they there? The question is discomforting for everyone. If
these bodies are meant really to be representative of the
communities they serve or of the professions they employ or
of the taxpayer whose resources they spend, then they are no
more than the residence of conflicting interests, some of
which cannot be reconciled. If they are primarily managerial,
then they commonly have only a modest competence at best
but even more importantly have only weak instruments with
which to command and control the resources and services for
which they are nominally responsible—and which exclude
many of high importance. Some fresh thinking is called for.

Secondly, there is the distorted and distorting pyramid of
power: ultimate responsibility remains vested in the Secretary
of State (of whom there are four individuals at any one time in
different parts of the UK). This has over the years led to an
increasing expectation that the Secretary of State, which
means a small group of Ministers and senior officials in the
centre, will 'manage the service'—with only a vague idea of
what the words 'manage' and 'service' mean—and, by
implication, be responsible for making good any deficiency.
For so long as Exchequer funding remains the main or only
source of money, that expectation will remain. But it cannot
be 'managed' in any meaningful sense of the term at this level

and, in any case, many key aspects of national health care remain outside the pyramid of Authorities which skews the sense of priorities. Perhaps even more important is the distorting effect on the pyramid itself of the assumption that uniformity is not only necessary but desirable. If this assumption were held and nourished only in the centre it would be dangerous enough, but it seems to have flourished in the institutions of 'the health service' as well, stifling initiative or perhaps more accurately, creating an environment in which initiatives require to be authorised or directed by the centre if they are not to be called out of order by local vested interests. Two examples come readily to mind: why did it occur to no one to find out whether a local firm could do, or help with, the laundry before building (with the blessing of the Department of course) the big centralised laundries? And why did it not occur to any Family Practitioner Committee to take the initiative in asking all its GPs and pharmacists to combine in an effort to identify those most at risk in the local population, particularly the elderly? We should all be concerned at the debilitating effect on any local sense of responsibility of the assumption that this will always be 'the Government's' problem, and that its solution lies in the Government providing more money or a standard policy directive.

Thirdly, there is the lack of identity between the workforce and its employer. A large workforce working in hundreds of different locations, in thousands of distinguishable units or multi-disciplinary teams; an employer who is nominally local but does not determine his own budget or the numbers, terms, and conditions of services of his staff, or the demands on them; competing unions which have an interest of their own in maintaining central responsibility for personnel matters; and that central responsibility having to be discharged in a party political context under the ultimate direction of Ministers —all of these combine to produce not just turbulence but disaffection. It is too easy to write the problem off as insoluble. The armed forces and the conglomerate plcs offer countless examples of how to turn these constraints so that leadership can be given by authority, and ·those under direction can positively identify with the team they are working in. The

Management Review was right to highlight the personnel function as the key to better management of the hospital service—and its Chairman was right to describe the task than as a lifetime's work for a young man. We have barely begun.

The drift of all this is obvious: beware the monolith, flee the paralysing demand for uniformity; encourage the search to find new resources of one's own. The prevailing winds are always adverse, in the sense that the giver of the taxpayer's money will be under a perpetual obligation to follow it through to the point of expenditure, to question the value obtained and to make comparisons of performance in seemingly comparable situations: in brief, to interfere Parliament itself will therefore need to think more deeply about its role so as to accept less uniformity, rigidity, and constraint in the bodies for whom it votes resources. The recipient authority which is wholly dependant on the taxpayer will always have the alibi of too little money and too much interference; and the incentive to use that alibi by a public clamouring for more and better. It should have freedom to help itself and an expectation that it will do so.

We shall, necessarily, go on wrestling with these intractables for decades. There is no quick structural solution available. And whatever shifts may emerge from or be canvassed in the current review will necessarily take the health care system into a prolonged period of transition if they are really thought through and well managed. If they are not, they will leave some of the intractables untouched and create confusion.* There are no blinding insights or flashes of inspiration which I can offer but these reminiscences and reflections have brought home to me four aspects which seem essential for the betterment of our care of the national health.

---

* To those who think otherwise I commend the three resolutions of the Church elders in one of the Southern States of America on the eve of the Civil War.

Resolved, we shall build a new school house.

Resolved, it shall be built on the same site as the old house, using so much as can be of its materials.

Resolved, the present school house shall remain in use to teach the children until the new house is ready.

First, and the most important requirement is that we see the whole and be not preoccupied with one part, however big, costly, and important, to the exclusion of others which may ultimately be even more crucial to the health and well-being of the population. We should recognise that it is asking too much of a few Ministers and senior officials to do this—the financial and Parliamentary pressures and their proper responsibilities of management however narrowly defined, will overload them anyway. Health care uniquely requires a national multi-disciplinary and open forum outside Government, but able to speak directly to it, which can address the whole and assess the implications objectively, with authority but never with passion, political or professional.

Secondly, I reflect that the human beings engaged in the delivery of health care are essentially no different from the millions who have shown over the last 15 years that they have immense reserves of individual initiative still untapped; and that it is so often released to great effect when authority and responsibility is identified with ownership. Be it jogging, walking, or moderation in eating and drinking to care for one's body; be it the refurbishment of owner-occupied council houses; be it the slow awakening to customer needs of the public utility leviathans—the examples are too pervasive to allow that 'the National Health Service' (whatever that is) is different.

'Privatisation' or 'contracting out' or 'competitive tendering' are not the words I would use to develop this point, although each has played its part, in the health care system as well as elsewhere. Other models will emerge, including I hope, the transfer of public assets, the grant-aid to run them, and the responsibility for their use to Trusts and Trustees or bodies like them who would make no pretence of being what they are not, but could combine ownership and authority with independence and the responsibility to use and raise more of their resources with vigour and imagination.

Thirdly, I look for a smaller and clearer role for the central Departments of State in caring for the national health. It is right that Parliament should hold Ministers and the Accounting Officers to account. But the combined effect of the ever-expanding Parliamentary requirement and the oppressive central obligation to secure 'efficiency' at the operating level is to squeeze out the essential role—which must belong to Government—of *thinking*, assessing the present policies and prospecting for better and more relevant policies for the future. 'If the new civil service (i.e. the management-orientated civil service created out of the Financial Management Initiative) cannot find a place for policy analysis, the functioning of the public service both as a provider of some services and the regulator of the private sector may become superbly efficient but it will certainly not be as effective as it should be.'*

Lastly, since I started with management in my brief, let me end with it, to make a very simple point. The able manager will be needed in the health care system in all disciplines and at all levels but there is more to it than the prescription of his or her essential qualities and qualifications, important though these are. What is also needed is that *the job is able to be managed*. The impossible will not be done by people of normal capacity, or even exceptional capacity, on a grand scale. And we require our health care system to operate on a very grand scale indeed. The manager must in Sir Michael Edwardes' words, 'be able to get his arms round the tree'. Our trees are too big in the health care business; and the management revolution which was seen to be required will not come about unless the demands on the people running it at all levels are made manageable, which means essentially giving them a clear field of responsibility, with a 'do-able' job to account for and the freedom to make the best of it.

I see no immediately obvious grand design to give effect to these considerations but I do yearn for experiment, and for the creation of an environment for the health care system as a whole which expects and demands innovation, experiment, and evaluation. The medical profession is, after all, the supreme example where that expectation is built in from initial training to the consultant appointment and which

* Mrs G. T. Banks, Registrar-General in a paper to the joint RIPA and PA Consulting Group Seminar on Performance Management.

combines science and its discipline with individuality, leadership and an ethical commitment to the patients. The health care system should follow suit.

# Postscript

These essays were completed before, and in ignorance of the Government's White Paper setting out its conclusions on the review of 'The Health Service'. A few further reflections may be in order.

It would be easy—but probably misguided—to criticise the White Paper for what it is not. It is not an appraisal of 40 years of caring for the national health: the betterment in the health of the population at large is barely touched on, in nineteen words, in the first paragraph. And they rightly claim only that the health service 'contributed' to the advances in life expectancy and infant mortality. A cleaner and safer environment at home and at work; healthier life styles; major developments in pharmaceuticals—these too have contributed. There is undoubtedly need for a comprehensive appraisal from time to time of progress, or lack of it, in caring for the national health. No one Government Department or Minister is competent to undertake it and it is in any event better done outside Government (43). The case for a National Council or Institute of Health—independent of Government, objective, unblinkered and authoritative—to lead on these matters remains as strong as ever. An initiative is needed—not from the Government and not financed by the Exchequer.

'Working for Patients' is—leaving the political rhetoric aside—primarily about the further development of the management process in the hospital services. As such it is carrying forward the Government's Financial Management Initiative (here called the Resource Management Initiative), which has for the past seven years been establishing management budgeting and management accounting in the Central Government Departments. This process had already begun in

Notes begin on page 90

the hospital service and it will be as long and hard a slog to carry it through, as it has been and still is in Central Government. The critical path to good progress lies in the accurate and full costing of inputs; in a usable management information system covering both costs and activities (with the technology to support it); in the establishment of performance criteria embracing what in the private sector is commonly called Total Quality Management and which here must, of course, embrace medical audit; and above all in the acceptance by those whose decisions on patients commit resources, of responsibility for the management of the whole. There are good models, with proven systems and methods already available, both in the private sector and in health care institutions overseas, especially in New England and New Zealand. We should not find it impossible in the UK.

None of this merits much in the way of political hyperbole, for or against. It is main-stream stuff. And all the better for that. If the medical profession embraces the opportunities now open to lead a massive upgrading in the general level of hospital care, with the necessary resources of skilled people that good management requires, we shall achieve a major advance—in ten years rather than the three specified in the Government's published timetable. But good trees always take longer to grow than weeds.

What is radical in the White Paper, and long overdue, is first, a willingness to break the monolithic structure and to make a modest start at least on dumping some of the structural garbage. No tears need be shed for the hundreds of Health Authority appointees, whether from Local Government or elsewhere, who might depart the system. No one could ever see precisely why they were there. Nor should we weep for RAWP*. It was a relic of the era when a centrally-planned economy was thought to be the natural order of things and public expenditure could be managed in real terms; i.e. pretending that real money was a marginal refinement in the system. It is that philosophy of central planning and control

---

* The formula devised by the Resource Allocation Working Party to 'equalise' hospital provision at a uniform national standard.

which has created the monolithic structure. We all now know that it does not work, because it cannot generate at the periphery, where services are delivered, the energy and initiative necessary for success (44).

Secondly, and even more important, is the acceptance and promotion of diversity in institutions, in the shape of Trust-owned and managed hospitals with the freedom to buy and sell services to meet the needs of the community they serve. The crucial test here is whether Parliament will enact the necessary legislation in a form which gives the Trusts freedom to take any action they deem appropriate to secure the resources and services required to carry out their obligation. The more detail in the Act or Regulations, the dimmer the prospect.

Finally, and potentially most radical of all, is the identification of the general practitioner chosen freely by the patient as his surrogate purchaser of hospital services and, coupled with this, the ability of the general practitioner—who chooses the consultant he thinks best—to send the money with the patient. This, of course, depends upon the general practitioners' responding with enthusiasm and skill to the offer for larger group practices to acquire their own budgets; and upon their being convinced that the budgets will be adequate and the performance criteria reasonable.

Perestroika? Perhaps. But much turns on Parliament, the Public Accounts Committee and the National Audit Office. A pre-occupation on their part with detail and superficially comparative measures of performance could clog the system with defensive bureaucracy. Of course, fifty-fold variations in standards of performance are intolerable. No variation at all is, however, unattainable and its pursuit is dangerous. Freedom to act means freedom to differ in judgement and act accordingly.

Much turns too on the many dialogues that must now take place between the Government and what the White Paper coyly describes as 'interested parties'. Here there is need of wisdom and wise counsel. As so often, the Scots seem to get the tone right:

> 'It is doctors, not politicians or managers, who treat patients and the Government is therefore seeking the full co-operation of the profession.'

There is indeed no alternative.

As Francis Bacon put it nearly four centuries ago in his essay 'Of Negociating':

> 'In all Negociations of Difficultie, a Man may not look to Sowe and Reape at once: But must prepare Businesse, and so Ripen it by Degrees.'

# NOTES

1. I gave some account of this in my lecture to the Royal Society for the Encouragement of Arts, Manufacturers and Commerce on The Management of a Great Department of State (*RSA Journal*, October 1986).

2. Tuberculosis was the single most important cause of death among adults in Britain before the Second World War. Now it has joined smallpox, and polio, for example, as diseases which have been or can be largely prevented or eradicated, and it has ceased to be a major cause of death. Changes like this lead on to one of the great imponderables of health care provision: what addition if any should be made in each year's allocation of resources for the *extra* cost of medical advance? Received thinking in the 1980s has been that 0·5 per cent more per annum is needed for Health Authority budgets to cover this. This curiously precise figure takes account of the off-setting savings of medical advance, e.g. in not having to treat so many ulcers by surgery. But it only brought home to me what an unscientific field 'health economics' is. A patient under the age of fifty not now needing treatment, or much treatment, for a previously killing or disabling disease, swells the number of those who, in their eighties, are the most expensive of all to care for. I have never regarded 'medical advance' as more than a tactical argument.

3. The IMF's aid was sought by the UK Government in the Autumn of 1977 to assist the recovery from severe inflation coupled with a depreciation of sterling in world markets and an outflow of capital which brought the economy to the brink of disaster. The price of the IMF loans was a much tighter fiscal and monetary policy and a very substantial reduction in public expenditure to take immediate effect. The public expenditure provision for health care, including the hospital building capital programme, was necessarily hit by those measures, thus beginning a decade of controversy about its funding.

4. There are two studies which should be compulsory reading for all who, hereafter, have to wrestle with these matters. The Rock Carling monograph *Reflections on the Universities and the National Health Service* by Sir Fred (now Lord) Dainton FRS; and the historical introduction in Chapter 1 (Incessant construction) of Professor Charles Webster's *The Health Services Since the War*. I cannot better Lord Dainton's perception of the harsh reality on p. 110 of his volume; my family shared in it.

5. For those interested I should explain that there are only two ways of defining 'a poverty line'. The first is to establish the cash value of the essential requirements of life, food, warmth, clothing, and shelter by

reference to an 'absolute' standard. The second is to establish the level of income below which an individual or family would be in poverty relative to the population at large. Beveridge's approach was neither: it was not original but based on a series of increments to all the earlier essays in this field. I traced them back to the Poor Law Regulation of the late 19th Century and then gave up. The problem of rent (which wrecked the early flat-rate national insurance benefit system and led on to the supplementary benefit and housing benefit schemes) was addressed in a similarly backward looking and superficial manner.

6. The current National Insurance contribution for an employee contracted in to the SERPS is 9 per cent gross earnings up to the upper earnings limit; the National Health element of this is 0·85 per cent. It yields only £27m p.a. (1987–88) towards the total UK public expenditure budget for the NHS of £20.·8 bn. There is, of course, a strong economic case made by the Treasury against a 'hypothecated tax' of any kind, and a universal NHI contribution would have been and still would be just that. But so, of course, is a NI contribution. It is of interest that Beveridge's original thinking was more flexible: thus the Insurance Fund was expected to make a substantial grant towards the medical service and, as the representative of the consumer, have a major voice in the administration of the Health Service; hotel charges for in-patients, and charges for subsidiary services were also considered; and he favoured inducements for workers to continue their voluntary contributions to ensure survival of the voluntary hospitals (Webster, op cit p. 36).

7. The illusion dies hard. When the appointment of Mr Duncan Nicholl as Chief Executive of the NHS Management Board was announced, this admirable step was greeted by 'authoritative' sources in the Health Authorities as a step towards defeating 'the Civil Service hi-jacking of the NHS Management Board' (*Independent*, 1 December 1988). In fact, as a senior civil servant accountable to Ministers and the Accounting Officer for the HCHS Votes, his obligations to Parliament would be the same as his predecessor's.

8. A distinction has to be made here between health education as such and the responsibility of Government to give clear advice and even instruction to the public on public health hazards, e.g. that a certain food product has been found to be contaminated and should not be eaten (an event that occurs fairly regularly) or that a particular product has been found to be unsafe. In practice health education and public health control can overlap. But the general principle still holds that Government should so far as possible avoid involvement in matters which mix medical science and personal behaviour with imprecision.

9. Good government has not, of course, been helped by the variety of bodies which exercise their lungs on the medical aspects of food manufacture and consumption. At the centre, working for the public interest and reporting to Ministers, is the Committee on Medical Aspects of Food Policy (COMA), an expert committee chaired by the Chief Medical

Officer, with further expert sub-committees and panels to pursue particular subjects or problems and prepare reports which Ministers can publish. But there are other independent bodies and every sector of the food manufacturing industry has its own representative body and/or lobby. The issue of salmonella in eggs was a spectacular illustration of interests in conflict and Government confused.

10. On the best information available there are approximately 2900 product licences in existence for products available for sale over the counter (OTC). There are also approximately another 2900 product licences in existence for products available for sale subject to the approval of a qualified pharmacist. These figures do not, of course, include products available only on prescription.

11. My nearest village pharmacy stocks 35 of these different leaflets on public display. The Medicines Commission has no role in relation to these leaflets unless they include information on specific products. They have a more important role in stimulating the production of good intelligible notes for the patient on dosage, method, etc., to be associated with the medicines supplied to him. The Association for British Pharmaceutical Industry has taken this further by publishing to its members guidance on the drafting of leaflets for patient information.

12.1 An independent Committee under the Chairmanship of Sir Kenneth Clucas KCB produced *Pharmacy: A report to the Nuffield Foundation* (The Nuffield Foundation, 1986). The committee's terms of reference were: 'To consider the present and future structure of the practice of pharmacy in its several branches and its potential contribution to health care, and to the review the education and training of pharmacists accordingly.' Among its recommendation were: 20. There is scope for transferring some medicines from the Prescription Only Medicines (POM) to the Pharmacist category under suitable safeguards. 21. The General Sales list should remain. The pharmacist should not be given a monopoly but should compete through quality of service.

12.2 A Departmental Committee chaired by Mrs Julia Cumberlege, now Chairman S.W. Thames Regional Health Authority, produced *Neighbourhood Nursing—A focus for care:* A report of the Community Nursing Team for England (HMSO, 1986). The terms of reference were: 'To study the nursing services provided outside hospital by Health Authorities and to report to the Secretary of State on how resources can be used more effectively, so as to improve the services available to client groups. The input from nurses employed by general practitioners will be taken into account.' Among its recommendations were: 7. The DHSS should agree a limited list of items and simple agents, which may be prescribed by nurses as part of a nursing care programme, and issue guidelines to enable nurses to control drug dosage in well-defined circumstances.'

13. I understand that the idea was considered of nationalising one major

pharmaceutical company, to exploit the market in the 'national interest', but it was dropped.

14. The Pharmaceutical Price Regulation Scheme (PPRS), in operation since the late 1950s, regulates NHS pharmaceutical prices by controls on the level of profit that pharmaceutical manufacturers make on their NHS business. The scheme is non-statutory and has two objectives: reasonable prices for NHS medicines and the encouragement of a strong and innovative UK pharmaceutical industry. Under the scheme, which covers branded medicines; the 90 or so participating companies make returns to the Department of Health of their aggregate NHS supply costs and capital employed; the Department satisfies itself that the costs claimed are properly attributable to NHS business; the target profitability for each company is set, expressed as a return on the capial invested in NHS business. The rate for each company varies within a set range, depending mainly on the Department's assessment of companies' UK operation and the risks they incur through manufacturing, investment and Research and Development; extra profits may be negotiated by companies achieving significant innovation or efficiency. The PPRS provides control on the aggregate costs and profits of each company. Companies have considerable freedom in the pricing of individual medicines. The Scheme does not restrict what medicines will be available to the NHS and any company can introduce a new product to the market, subject to a product licence being obtained.

15. The PAC's hearing of evidence on the pharmaceutical services from me (as Accounting Officer) and my colleagues is fully recorded in their Tenth Report of the 1982–83 session.

16. The League of Friends of Rampton Hospital (a hospital for the secure care and treatment of mentally ill and/or handicapped adults with violent behavioural problems) provide, for example, travel and visiting facilities for the relatives of these pathetically isolated patients. The Salvation Army's hostel in Limehouse for the homeless accommodates a detoxification unit giving real community care under their own clinical and professionally qualified staff. The blood-donor system provides the best and most secure supply in the world of blood for hospital use, depending upon donations from some 1·5 million individuals each year. The hospital car service provides cars and their drivers at no cost to the Health Authorities other than the mileage allowance for petrol, etc., and a modest subsistence payment for their drivers. It is of interest that the Department holds no information about this service! The hospice movement, starting from the inspired developments at the Roman Catholic Foundation in Hackney (St Joseph's Hospice), and at St Christopher's in Sydenham, is now established throughout the country in at least 72 locations—even more importantly, its ideals of care are being transferred belatedly into hospitals, residential and nursing homes, and into home care services.

17. The differences in 'NHS' costs per head of population in the early, middle, and late age-ranges are striking:

*Health and Personal Social Services estimated gross current expenditure per head per annum by age-group (England) 1986–87.*

|  | £ per head |  | £ per head |
|---|---|---|---|
| All ages | 360 | 16–64 years | 205 |
| Birth | 1,300 | 65–74 | 615 |
| 0–4 years | 370 | 75 and over | 1,570 |
| 5–15 | 255 |  |  |

The projected growth in numbers of the old makes the point even clearer:

*Projected growth in numbers over 70 and over 85 UK) up to 2,025*

|  | Over 70 '000 | Over 85 '000 |  | Over 70 '000 | Over 85 '000 |
|---|---|---|---|---|---|
| 1985 | 4,761 | 615 | 2010 | 4,835 | 1,188 |
| 1990 | 4,737 | 761 | 2015 | 5,032 | 1,200 |
| 1995 | 4,928 | 921 | 2020 | 5,699 | 1,186 |
| 2000 | 4,919 | 1,044 | 2025 | 5,940 | 1,219 |
| 2005 | 4,891 | 1,072 |  |  |  |

(OPCS, Projected populations by age last birthday, Mid-1985 based)

The scale of the problem is indicated by the fact that one-in-five of the over-80s is judged now to be suffering from senile dementia (Alzheimer's Disease).

18. *Residential Care: A positive choice*. Report of the Independent Review of Residential care HMSO, 1988).

19. The Report of the House of Lords Select Committee on Science and Technology on Priorities in Medical Research gives these broad figures— they are not precise since they mix UK and England figures—and in any case omit the medical schools' UGC contribution.

| MRC | £121·5m |
|---|---|
| Medical research charities | £110·0m |
| Pharmaceutical Industry | £490·0m |
| DHSS | £17·8m (1985–86 figures) |

20. The Health Services Research programme enjoys its own published annual report on projects approved by the Department of Health. I have to record that it was not avidly read by Ministers or senior officials.

21. A Framework for Government Research and Development. Cmnd 4814.

22. *Committee of Inquiry into Human Fertilisation and Embryology*, published July 1984. Cmd 9314.

23. A good example is the market research into young people's attitudes commissioned by the Division concerned with how best to counter the growing tendency to smoke among young people.

24. These do not, of course, necessarily equate with Ministers' priorities

or concerns but may influence them. Some health services research was commissioned which did, however, serve strategic purposes. Two good examples are: (1) In 1985 an extensive University research project funded by the DHSS reached the conclusion that the heart transplant programme provided good value for money, and the programme was subsequently expanded on the basis of this finding. There is little doubt that without such objective research the heart transplant programme would have been seriously curtailed. (2) The abandonment of the Bonham Carter Committee's proposals to *increase* the size of District General Hospitals—a good illustration of the power of research to guide policy in the right direction.

But the dismal fact remains, as the House of Lords Select Committee on Science and Technology discovered (*Priorities in Medical Research*. Third Report, 1987–88 Chapter 2), that the connection between health services research and the formulation of government policy is minimal.

25. The 200 District-based CHCs were set up under the Reorganisation of the NHS Act 1973, primarily to represent the interests in the health service of the public in their districts.

26. The Institute of Cancer Research, for example, which is related to the Royal Marsden Hospital receives no funds directly from the University of London but is wholly funded by voluntary donations, including a large proportion from the Cancer Research Campaign, and by grants from the MRC.

27. The Resource Allocation Working Party (RAWP) was set up in 1975 'to review the arrangements for distributing NHS capital and revenue (to Health Authorities), with a view to establishing a method of securing, as soon as practicable, a pattern of distribution responsive objectively, equitably and efficiently to relative need, and to make recommendations'. The Working Party developed criteria for equity in resource allocation and, since it found substantial disparities between regions, recommended methods of allocating resources more equitably.

For revenue purposes, the RAWP formula is used to calculate target (or fair) shares of national allocation for the hospital and community health services. The formula is concerned with the overall allocation, not with patterns of expenditure. The Working Party recognised that Authorities cannot cope efficiently with very large decreases or increases in expenditure and that redistribution must be gradual.

The distinctive feature of the RAWP formula was relative need, based on factors including size of population (weighted to reflect differences in population make-up since different age/sex groups make greater or lesser use of different health services) and Standard Mortality ratios (the number of deaths which actually occurred in a particular region, in relation to the national average). Adjustments are made to take account of patient flows across regional boundaries to receive treatment and separate increments are added where appropriate to reflect added costs in London regions or in teaching hospitals.

Since 1975, a number of adjustments have been made to the formula to ensure that the targets reflect need as fairly as possible but the basic principles have remained.

28. *Report on the Review of Rampton Hospital.* CM 8073 1980.

On 22 May 1979, a film was shown on independent television about Rampton Hospital in Nottinghamshire, one of four 'Special Hospitals' run by the Department of Health for persons detained under the Mental Health Act who in the opinion of the Secretary of State 'require treatment under conditions of special security on account of their dangerous, violent or criminal propensitites'. The film, entitled 'The Secret Hospital', contained a large number of serious allegations of ill-treatment of patients by staff.

Patrick Jenkins MP, the Secretary of State for Social Services, together with some senior officials from the Department, had seen a preview of the film and the day before the public screening, announced that he had referred the allegations of ill-treatment to the Director of Public Prosecutions, and had arranged for a full review of the organisation, management and facilities at Rampton Hospital (this was led by Sir John Boynton).

The report, published in November 1980, made wide-ranging recommendations for improvements to Rampton Hospital and the lives of the patients there, which were largely accepted. The hospital, and subsequently the other Special Hospitals, became subject to the supervision of independent boards of management drawn from outside the hospitals.

29. *McColl Report. Review of Artificial Limb and Appliance Centre Services. The Report of an independent working party under the chairmanship of Professor Ian McColl, 1986.*

30. This idea has a long and respectable history going back to the reconstruction of local government under the legislation of 1929 which was the springboard for major but uneven development of comprehensive health care services based on local hospitals owned and run by local authorities. See Webster, op. cit., pp 5 et seq; pp 84 et seq.

31. The social security item broke surface, of course, in the Griffiths Report on Community Care, having been crudely resuscitated in the Audit Commission report referred to in Chapter 9.

32. The Parliamentary Question announcing the annual review process, on 22 January 1982, ran as follows:

*Health Authorities (Accountability to Parliament)*

Mr du Cann asked the Secretary of State for Social Services what action he proposes to take in response to the comments in the seventeenth report from the Committee on Public Accounts about the need for greater accountability of English health authorities to Parliament.

'Mr Fowler: I am introducing new arrangements to ensure better accountability for the NHS. I believe that it is both desirable and practicable to secure the maximum delegation of responsibility for the delivery of local health services to District Health Authorities while at the same time achieving true accountability from the district authorities through the Regional Health Authorities.

Accordingly, each year Ministers will lead a departmental review of the long-term plans, objectives, and effectiveness of each region with the chairmen of the Regional Authorities and Chief Regional Officers. The aims of the new system will be to ensure that each Region is using the resources allocated to it in accordance with the Government's policies—for example, giving priority to services for the elderly, the handicapped and the mentally ill—and also to establish agreement with the chairmen on the progress and development which the Regions will aim to achieve in the ensuing year. Successive reviews will thus enable Ministers to measure the progress made by Regions against the agreed plans and objectives, as well as to determine action necessary in the year ahead.

The new system will be established in 1982–83. My Department is also conducting a pilot scheme in one Region using indicators of performance in the delivery of health services. These will enable comparison to be made between Districts, and so help Ministers and the Regional chairmen at their annual review meeting to assess the performance of their constituent District Health Authorities in using manpower and other resources efficiently. With these arrangements I shall be able to hold Regional Health Authorities to account for the ways in which resources are used in their regions and for the efficiency with which services are delivered. In turn, the regional health authorities will hold their constituent district health authorities to account.

The reviews will concentrate on major issues, leaving district health authorities with the primary responsibility for decision-taking in providing local operational services within agreed policies. In addition, in order to ensure that they have adequate influence over certain matters for which the regional health authorities are responsible—for example, the provision of regionally-managed support services—I have asked the RHAs for reports on the arrangements in the region for involving the districts in these matters.

The object of these new arrangements is to ensure that the Health Service obtains the maximum amount of direct patient care and the greatest value for money from the resources which the Government have made available to the NHS.'

33. *Health Service Indicators (HSIs)* cover the main service areas in the hospital and community health sector and enable Health Authorities critically to examine local performance in the national context. HSIs are not precise measures but provide clues about potential problems. A new set of indicators, known as 'Körner' indicators have been developed in consultation with the NHS, for issue early in 1989. (Mrs Körner, as Vice-Chairman, South Western RHA, led the Department's review of Health Service Statistics 1981–83). The new set contains approximately 2,500 indicators, taking account of all variants by specialty and age group. They will continue to be presented on computer; and existing presentation systems are being revised.

34. The late Albert Spanswick was General Secretary of the Confederation of Health Service Employees (COHSE) and Chairman of the TUC Health Services Committee. Peter Jacques was Secretary to this Committee.

35. The Griffiths recommendations were summarised in the implementation circular to Health authorities (HC(84)13). They are worth reproducing here as a reminder of what had to be done; and how much remains to do; and how much has been simply taken up anew in the 1989 White Paper:

ANNEX B
(HC(84)13)

### FURTHER PROGRAMME OF MANAGEMENT ACTION

The NHS Management Inquiry set out its recommendations in the form of a programme of management action to be taken both at the centre and by health authorities. The recommended programme is:

1. Policy of accountability for performance against agreed objectives should be maintained and developed.

2. Accountability reviews should be extended to units.

3. The management function should be developed
   a. inside the Department
   b. in the NHS.

4. Pilot projects in management budget techniques should be continued with the aim that they be extended to all health authorities in about 2/3 years.

5. 11 specific topics should be studied or reviewed
   the need for functional management structures at RHA/DHA
   the role of clinicians in management, in six hospitals
   the arrangements for remuneration etc
   the assessment of management training
   the procedures for appointments etc
   nurse manpower levels
   other manpower levels
   the procedures on capital schemes
   the works function
   levels of decision-taking
   consultation arrangements

6. The roles of members and officers in relation to their authorities should be clarified.

7. The agenda and the procedures for health authority meetings should be clarified and the nature of the reports required by the authority in managing its services should be made explicit.

8. Major cost-improvement programmes should be initiated in each health authority.

9. Each unit should have a total budget and have management accountant support.


### 36. The Membership of the NHSMB in 1985 was:

| | |
|---|---|
| Chairman | Mr Victor Paige |
| Director of Health Authority Finance | Mrs G T Banks |
| | Under Secretary, DHSS |
| Director of Planning and IT | Mr M Fairey |
| | Chairman of the Health Service Information Advisory Group |
| Director of Health Authority Liaison | Mr C Graham |
| | Under Secretary, DHSS Replaced later in 1985 by Mr A Merifield, also Under Secretary, DHSS |
| Director of Operations | Mr G Hart |
| | Deputy Secretary, DHSS |

| | |
|---|---|
| Director of Financial Management | Mr I mills<br>seconded to DHSS Senior Partner, Price Waterhouse |
| Director of Personnel | Mr L Peach<br>seconded to DHSS Director of Personnel, IBM |
| Chief Medical Officer | |
| Chief Nursing Officer | |
| Director of Procurement and Distribution | Mr T Critchley<br>Under Secretary, recruited from the private sector in purchasing |
| Part-time Property Advisor | Mr D N Idris Pearce<br>Senior Partner in Richard Ellis |
| Non-executive Director | Mr D Nicholl<br>RGM, Mersey RHA |

In June 1986, Mr Paige resigned as chairman of the NHSMB. The Rt Hon Tony Newton MP, the Minister for Health, became Chairman and Mr Len Peach, formerly Director of Personnel, became Chief Executive.

In September 1986, following a Ministerial reshuffle The Rt Hon Kenneth Clarke MP, Secretary of State for Health, took over the chairmanship.

37. *Dispensing of drugs in the NHS* Tenth report, 1982/3 session. HC356; *Dispensing of drugs in the NHS* Twenty ninth report, 1983/4 session. HC551; *NHS General Dental Service* Seventeenth report 1984/5 session. HC111; *Preventative medicine* Forty fourth report, 1985/86 session. HC 413.

38. The chastening experience of being summoned to appear in person to answer before this Select Committee of the House of Commons does not stop with the few individuals who had to obey this command. It concentrates the minds of their peers too—they might be next.

39. Patients are entitled to bring to the attention of health authorities aspects of their care and treatment about which they are unhappy. There are three possible stages. At the first, it is the responsibility of the consultant of the patient concerned to look into the complaint. Should the complainant be dissatisfied with the written reply, the second stage involves the Regional Medical Officer and such discussion as are appropriate, including one with the complainant. If this also fails to satisfy the complainant, the third stage is an Independent Professional Review, although this is only suitable for complaints of a serious nature and where legal proceedings are not likely. Following the review, a formal letter on behalf of the authority is sent to the complainant. Clinical complaints are not within the Commissioner's remit, but the Select Committee are able to require information from the Department on how complaints are dealt with on the other side of the clinical divide and to apply their own pressure for improvement. The growing and real threat of patient litigation for redress of their grievances against clinicians should be a powerful inducement to all concerned, and especially the professional authorities, to deal with complaints in an open

and positive way. Even more important is to conduct the relationship with the patient and/or relatives in such a manner as will relieve 'the patient's dilemma' in Sir Cecil's analysis.

40. What is remarkable, nevertheless, is how effective the Committee has been. A good example is its hearings on the Report on NHS Management, during which it pricked the bubble of some unsupported claims made against the idea of general management and supported the thrust of the reform.

41. It also requires a better framework than the existing system of public accounts. Although the accounts I regularly signed distinguished between the revenue and capital programmes of health authorities' expenditure there is this fundamental difference between them: the revenue expenditure will all be used in the year and, therefore, cease to be in the possession of authorities whereas the capital expenditure, *ipso facto*, adds to the value of the permanent assets. But the public accounts do not show the value of the capial assets, nor is their value known to those controlling them (their owner is, of course, the Secretary of State and he most certainly does not know!). A step in the right direction was the report of the Ceri Davies Committee of 1982–83 on the management of the estate, which (1) pointed to the need to put a value on all the estate and attribute the cost to the users as a first step towards its better management; and (2) assessed the backlog of maintenance which needed to be tackled to prevent the problem getting worse. The point is made simply enough in this context by the figures. The estate in England could be valued only approximately at £23 billion; and the crude estimate of the maintenance backlog was £2 billion.

42. 'The final (Beveridge) Report was less firm on the necessity for a free service. In sections omitted from the Brief Report, Beveridge considered the possibility of a 10 shilling hotel expenses charge for hospital patients and also charges for subsidiary services, as well as for dental and optical appliances.' Webster, op cit., p. 36.

43. It is in the nature of Government that Departments and their Ministers take at best a partial view and this will not do for health care. If, for example, the prevention of premature death remains a high priority objective, the onus for achieving progress would not lie exclusively in the Department of Health but also in the departments and industries responsible for food manufacture and processing, catering, vehicle safety, traffic engineering and traffic law enforcement. They are not all likely to be active in bringing their potential contribution to the notice of the public and Parliament.

44. For those still in doubt, I commend the lecture on 'The Economics of Perestroika' by Academician Aganbegyan, Head of the Economics Department of the USSR Academy, Chief Economic Adviser to Mikhail Gorbachev, published in *International Affairs*, Winter, 1987.